Developmental Psychology

SAGE COURSE COMPANIONS

KNOWLEDGE AND SKILLS *for* SUCCESS

Developmental Psychology

Carol Brown

⑤SAGE

Los Angeles • London • New Delhi • Singapore

First published 2008

SAGE Publications Ltd
1 Oliver's Yard
55 City Road
London EC1Y 1SP

SAGE Publications Inc.
2455 Teller Road
Thousand Oaks, California 91320

SAGE Publications India Pvt Ltd
B 1/I 1 Mohan Cooperative Industrial Area
Mathura Road
New Delhi 110 044

SAGE Publications Asia-Pacific Pte Ltd
33 Pekin Street #02-01
Far East Square
Singapore 048763

Library of Congress Control Number: 2007929488

British Library Cataloguing in Publication data

A catalogue record for this book is available from the British Library

ISBN 978-1-4129-3465-7
ISBN 978-1-4129-3466-4 (pbk)

Typeset by C&M Digitals (P) Ltd., Chennai, India
Printed in India at Replika Press Pvt Ltd
Printed on paper from sustainable resources

To Matt whom I will always love

and

for Paul and Tim, the two most special sons who have really taught me about developmental psychology. I love you both.

contents

Why use this course companion to developmental psychology?

This book is designed to help you succeed on your degree level psychology course. The aim is to provide you with a course companion that gives you a short cut to understanding the basics behind developmental psychology. It is about helping you gain the most from your degree level course, passing your examinations in psychology and helping you to achieve success in your assignments.

It has been designed and written to provide you, the reader, with an easy-to-navigate guide to the commonly taught curriculum in developmental psychology, and the ways of thinking and writing that your examiners will be looking for when they start to grade your work.

This companion is not to be used instead of a textbook or wider reading, but rather as a means of memorising content and familiarising yourself with the basics of the discipline when preparing for an examination or planning an assessed essay. The book will help you to structure and organise your thoughts, and will enable you to get the most from your textbooks and the other reading that you will do as part of your course. This companion is designed to point you in the direction of key thinkers and key ideas, and to give you the briefest of introductions to their work and how to put their work in context. It will point you in the direction of the most important readings and thinkers, and will encourage you to widen your reading and research so as to improve your attainment.

The guide therefore provides you with ways of applying the information you are familiar with in a practical manner and is aimed at ensuring you gain the skills necessary to convey your theoretical/academic material successfully.

As you are still relatively new to the study of psychology you may assume that simply learning the material presented in lectures secures high achievement, but actually the learning and rewriting of information will not in fact gain you top marks. Instead you need to go beyond simply understanding the material and think critically about the research presented to you. This ability to evaluate theories/studies is the essential skill for becoming a successful psychologist.

Summary

Using this course companion will help you:

- understand the key theories/studies within developmental psychology, along-side your notes and wider reading
- highlight the skills necessary to pass this module by providing tips on answering questions and specifying running themes within topics.

How to use this book

This book should be used as a supplement to your textbook and lecture notes. You may want to glance through it quickly, reading it in parallel with your course syllabus and textbook, and note where each topic is covered in both the syllabus and this *Companion*. Ideally you should have already bought this book before your course starts, so that you can get a quick overview of each topic before you go into the lecture – but if you didn't do this, all is not lost. The *Companion* will still be equally helpful as a revision guide, and as a way of directing you towards the key thinkers and theories in developmental psychology.

Part One is about how to think like a developmental psychologist: it will help you to get into the mindset of the subject and think about it critically. As a bonus, of course, it also means learning how to think like your examiner! Examiners want to see that you can handle the basic concepts of your subject: if you need a quick overview of the background to developmental psychology, this is the section you will find most useful.

Part Two goes into the curriculum in more detail, taking each topic and providing you with the key elements. Again, this does not substitute for the deeper coverage you will have had in your lectures and texts, but it does provide a quick revision guide, or a 'primer' to use before lectures.

You can also use this book either to give yourself a head start before you begin studying developmental psychology – in other words give yourself a preview course – or as a revision aid, or of course both. Each section contains within it the following features:

- **Tips** on handling the information in exams, or reminders of key issues. These will help you to anticipate exam questions, and to remember the main points to bring in when answering them.
- **Examples** that are useful for putting theory into a 'real world' context, and can of course be used in exams to illustrate the points you make.
- **Running themes** of the areas that will always be of interest to a social psychologist. You will find that these can almost always be brought into an exam question, and you will be expected to do so.
- Input from **key thinkers** in the field, which will be useful to quote in exams, as well as providing you with the main influences and theories within cognitive psychology.
- Sample **exam questions** with outline **answers**. These should help you be better prepared for the actual questions, even though they will (of course) be different.
- The **textbook guide** is about taking your thinking a stage further and this section introduces some texts which focus on academic thinking, and will help you to take a broader conceptual view of the topic: on a practical level, this is the type of thinking that moves you from a pass to a first!

Part Three of the *Companion* is a study guide which will help you to get more from your lectures, to remember more when you are sitting exams, and to write essays.

The final section includes a glossary of the key terms used in the book and a list of references.

part one
the basics of developmental psychology

The overall aim of this part is to familiarise you with the basics of developmental psychology. It will:

- define developmental psychology as a topic
- provide an outline of developmental psychology and its related disciplines
- give you a brief history of developmental psychology
- introduce the founding figures and their core ideas
- encourage you to think like a developmental psychologist
- help you understand the general principles of assessment and expected learning outcomes when studying this area of psychology
- provide tips and examples of the running themes you will find throughout the text.

1.1
definition

Developmental psychology looks at the changes we go through as we get older and examines the key stages that influence all aspects of our development from the foetus, through infancy and then transitions into adolescence and adulthood. It covers a range of developmental areas including physical, social, emotional, cognitive and language development as well as relationships with wider social agents such as peers and family.

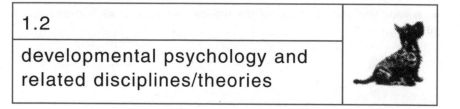

Many of these areas are interchangeable ones and may be the result of nature or nurture, that is, the result of biological factors or environmental ones.

1.2
developmental psychology and related disciplines/theories

Biology

Since humans are biological creatures there is an inevitable overlap between physical functioning and the developmental process. For example it looks at heredity, genes, embryology and pre-natal development. The link between the two areas is evident in the apparent interaction between biological/physical development and childhood growth, and explicit links can be seen in the sections on physical/motor development and on the influences of biology/heredity on behaviour.

Cognitive psychology

Cognitive psychology deals with topics such as perception, memory, attention, language and thinking/decision-making. Most critically it is based on the idea that we are like a computer when processing information and have input, storage and retrieval functions. Experimental cognitive psychology presumes that cognitive processes can be tested using empirical (scientific) methods because they can be inferred from behaviour obtained under controlled conditions. Introspection can however also be used whereby one examines one's own mental processes. The development of cognitive development generally, and areas such as perception and language in particular, are key sections in this current text.

Social psychology

Social psychology is about understanding individual behaviour in a social context. Baron, Byrne and Suls (1989) define it as 'the scientific field that seeks to understand the nature and causes of individual behaviour in social situations'. It therefore looks at human behaviour as influenced by other people and the context in which this occurs. Social psychologists deal with the factors that lead us to behave in a given way in the presence of others, and looks at the conditions under which certain behaviour/actions and feelings occur. It is to do with the way these feelings, thoughts, beliefs, intentions and goals are constructed and how such psychological factors, in turn, influence our interactions with others. This developmental text looks at how our development is aided/influenced by parents, peers and play, for example, and also at the development of gender.

Comparative psychology

The comparison between animal and human behaviour underlies this area of psychology, and the debate between the inheritance of species-specific behaviour patterns (phylogeny) and behaviour which is acquired during the species lifetime but is not shared with every member, is a running theme throughout this text. Perhaps most notably the concepts of imprinting and attachment behaviour highlighted in section 2.10 relate to this.

Although developmental psychology draws on the contribution of social, comparative and cognitive psychology, and biology, it is unique in its consideration of all of these disciplines when looking at development from a lifespan perspective.

1.3

history of developmental psychology

In any examination or essay you will be expected to know something about where developmental psychology comes from. This may simply be a matter of demonstrating a general understanding or not getting your origins muddled, but you may well be asked to write directly on the history of the discipline.

> *Understanding something of the history of developmental psychology will be crucial in helping you think like a developmental psychologist.*

Key developments

- 1882 – Wilhelm Preyer produced *The Mind of a Child* (translated into English, 1888) which was a rigorous case study of his own daughter's development, including observational records.
- 1894 – Alfred Binet founded the first scientific journal in this area (*L'année Psychologique*).
- 1891 – Stanley Hall founded a further journal – *Pedagogical Seminary*.
- 1890s – the first research institutes were set up in developmental psychology.
- 1905 – Binet published an intelligence test (Binet–Simon scale) which provided insight and guidance on the intellectual capabilities and potential of those suffering from mental retardation.
- 1915 – J.M. Baldwin published *Genetic Logic*, which introduced the concept that knowledge grows through childhood in a series of distinct stages, from initial physical development to language and cognitive abilities. This is believed to occur as an interaction between innate abilities and environmental feedback, such that the child emerges as a result of social and physical growth.
- 1916 – the Stanford–Binet test was produced which facilitated intelligence testing in children more widely.

As we will go now go on to see, the work of Jean Piaget, Lev Vygotsky and John Bowlby then ensured the true establishment of the developmental psychology field.

1.4
founding figures and their core ideas

The core ideas of the founding figures had either a philosophical influence (their ideas and beliefs impacted on thinking about developmental psychology) or a methodological influence (their ways of working and research studies influenced the development and thinking about developmental psychology).

Karl Ernst von Baer (1792–1876) – challenged the existing ideas that development follows a predetermined course as characteristics are already set at birth (preformationism), or that it moves through various stages which imitate that of the adult form of the species from which it has evolved (recapitulationism). Instead he introduced the idea that development occurs in stages, allowing for individual characteristics to emerge from more general ones.

Charles Darwin (1809–1882) – Darwin's evolutionary theory paved the way for the idea that development occurs as the child gradually adapts to its environment. He also introduced the notion that systematic and scientific methods could be used to study such development.

Jean Piaget (1896–1980) – was influenced by early theorists Binet and Baldwin (see above). He used a clinical approach to look at the systematic cognitive errors children made, in an attempt to understand something of a child's acquisition of knowledge and intellectual development. He initially proposed that the interaction of babies with their environment paved the way for thinking and language patterns. As we shall see later in this book he went on to propose a comprehensive theory combining evolutionary perspectives with the acquisition of knowledge as a biological process. This worked on the premise that babies are all born with similar biological properties and reflexes which mature to a state of 'readiness' whereby new information or experiences that cannot be assimilated challenge and then change a child's thinking.

Lev Vygotsky (1896–1934) – was also influenced by the early work of Baldwin and Binet. He focused, however, on cultural input, suggesting that this was the critical factor that transforms experience from a basic elementary function to a higher-order one. Rather than looking at fixed stages of development he focused (particularly) on the interaction between language and thought, assuming them to be separate functions before the age of two, after which time language and cultural tools facilitate problem-solving and social interaction.

John Bowlby (1907–1990) – Bowlby believed a mother and child form an innate monotrophic bond and that maternal deprivation occurs when the bond is broken in some way. He saw attachment as a two-way, genetic process that provides a child with a secure base from which to explore the world. He therefore stated that if maternal deprivation occurred then there would be irreversible long-term emotional consequences for the child. These include affectionless psychopathy in which the individual is unable to establish normal emotional development and experiences no feelings of emotion or guilt if carrying out crimes. The psychopath lacks affection and is unable to establish lasting relationships as an adult.

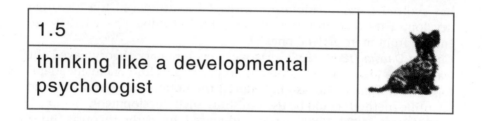

1.5

thinking like a developmental psychologist

The key to success in your developmental psychology module is to learn how to think like a developmental psychologist, including how to speak the language of academic psychology, using their terms and phrases in a relevant way and understanding how to make links between topics and common themes. This book will give you hints and tips to guide you. It will ensure that you become confident about when and how to use this language and the ways of thinking about the world that come with this language. This will be the focus of both this section and more specifically of part two.

This initial part of the book has introduced some of the basics of developmental psychology by helping you understand that it involves looking at development over the lifespan and at the influences upon such development. It also emphasised the notion that this needs to be done in a scientific way, and so to truly understand how to think like a developmental psychologist you will need first to understand more about this.

- *Scientific method* means that you need to test a hypothesis to examine variables that influence behaviour. Thus the hypothesis states that two variables are related in some way and if you alter one of them this may cause the participant to alter the other. In psychology we are trying to show that our results are significant and due to the thing we have changed (called the independent variable) rather than due to chance.

In order to think like a developmental psychologist you therefore need to understand clearly what a hypothesis is and what the role of variables is.

A hypothesis should be a precise, testable statement of a relationship between two or more variables.

There are two types of variables that should be included in each hypothesis:

- An **independent variable** (IV). This is the thing that the researcher *deliberately manipulates* so it is the thing that she purposely changes.
- A **dependent variable** (DV). This is what one hopes alters as a result of what is *changed* (so the DV measures any changes the IV has produced).

Generally one variable (the IV) is altered to see what effect it has on another variable (the DV). This means that cause and effect are being measured.

The IV is the thing you are changing
The DV is the thing you are measuring

You also need to be aware that your hypothesis can be tested using both experimental and non-experimental methods.

The principal difference is that experiments involve looking at whether manipulating one variable (the IV) has an effect on what you are measuring (the DV) and can involve laboratory experiments or field experiments, for example. In the laboratory the researcher deliberately manipulates variables using standardised procedures (the same method each time). In a field experiment the researcher also deliberately manipulates the IV but does so in the participants' own natural environment.

In contrast non-experimental methods may be more viable within the social context since, often, studying behaviour in the real world becomes unnatural if transferred to the laboratory, and therefore a range of other methods may be required, including:

- **Case studies,** which focus on one individual and their behaviour, thoughts, feelings and experiences.
- **Correlations,** which measure the strength of the relationship between two variables; for example, they test if there is a relationship between two things. They *do not*, however, test cause and effect – so they do not say that one thing causes the other but simply say there is some relationship between two things.
- **Questionnaires,** which use various types of questions to make a quick and efficient assessment of people's attitudes and which contain fixed or open-ended questions (or both).
- **Observations,** which look at the behaviour of participants in various situations and see 'a relatively unconstrained segment of a person's freely chosen behaviour as it occurs' (Coolican, 1990: 60). These can be structured or unstructured but can be carried out in the participants' natural environment.

Such work also needs to be carried out according to ethical guidelines, and special note needs to be made of those concerning deception, informed consent, withdrawal, debriefing and protection of participants from harm.

> *Thinking like a developmental psychologist involves weighing up the costs and benefits of research to determine if anything valuable can be found.*

Once you understand what developmental psychology is and how it can be investigated you are half way to understanding the key principles which underpin this module.

So how do you think like a developmental psychologist?

- You need to understand the changes and consistencies in development during the lifespan from conception through to old age, focusing on how particular behaviours change as a result of age.
- It is not a discipline that looks at how you behave/process information in a collective way but instead takes an individual slant.

- To be a successful developmental psychologist you will need to learn how to consider the theories presented as a scientist, that is, to talk about development in the context of the research studies/theories.
- You will also need to be aware that developmental psychologists use scientific methods when studying people and their development, and that they can test their hypotheses in experimental or non-experimental ways provided that ethical guidelines are always met.

When studying any topic in developmental psychology, you need to be aware of how the above disciplines have influenced the thinking of developmental psychologists as this will help you understand their perspective/explanation of development.

You must also consider the methodology and the advantages/ disadvantages/ethics of the methods used, as this will help you evaluate their work.

1.6	
learning outcomes and assessment	

Learning outcomes

At the end of your developmental psychology module you should be able to:

- understand and describe the major theories and areas of research in developmental psychology;
- think critically about the key studies/theories;
- understand and be able to evaluate the methods used to research developmental psychology;
- relate the theories and thinking of developmental psychologists to child development;

- understand the basic history and development of developmental psychology;
- understand the relationship between developmental psychology and other psychological approaches.

Assessment

You will be assessed in a number of ways, including essay-writing, projects and discussion work. Put simply, there are two basic skills that you need to be a good psychologist and it is these that your examiners will look for when assessing you:

- Firstly, for your **knowledge** and **understanding** of psychological theories, concepts and studies. So you might give a definition of a psychological term, outline a theory or a particular study carried out.
- Secondly, your **evaluation** of a psychological theory/argument/study will be examined – this essentially requires you to say what is good or bad about a theory/argument/study and focuses on *how* a theory or idea can be supported by research and *how* it can be criticised by research.

If you simply write out the relevant study and state that it does support/ criticise a theory you will not gain marks. Your essay questions test more than your ability to memorise and rewrite information. Instead they ask you to show that you have considered both sides of an argument and been able to draw an overall conclusion – you therefore need to show explicitly *how* a piece of evidence supports or criticises a theory/idea. It is the 'why' that will gain you the higher marks both on this particular question and the paper generally. Put bluntly, this skill demonstrated in your answer is the single factor that will make a difference to achieving the lower or the higher grades in your psychology degree.

With regard to achieving the degree you are aiming for, the following broad criteria should apply:

- **70+ marks will give you a first-class honours degree,** whereby you show a clear, coherent and logical argument that (most importantly) demonstrates clearly the key arguments, concepts and studies and shows an ability to evaluate these critically. Such analysis needs to reflect original thought, must be related to the set question and must be well supported by scientific evidence gained by the application of your wider reading.
- **60–69 marks will give you an upper second-class honours degree,** and will require you to show a clear, coherent and logical argument with good performance in the areas above. The main difference here is that you display less originality of thought than that required for a first-class honours. So you show

a good grasp of concepts, the relationship between them and support your arguments accordingly with the application of wider reading.

- **50–59 marks will give you a lower second-class degree,** means you demonstrate an organised argument but one that has irrelevant material or omissions, and show a general grasp of concepts and logical argument. Content may not be directly related to the question and evaluations do not reflect original analysis. There is less evidence of wider reading.
- **40–49 marks would result in a third-class degree,** whereby you show a basic understanding of the main concepts and arguments in developmental psychology, but there are errors or omissions and debate may be unstructured and irrelevant. There would also be little evidence of original thought, little use of scientific evidence to support arguments and little evidence of wider reading.

As you can see from these criteria, some of the key skills you require in psychology are an important feature of this text. However remember that this book is not a replacement for the wider reading you need to gain top marks – it will simply supplement what you know.

1.7	
running themes	

There will be a number of common themes that will run throughout this book – no matter what topic you are studying, these 'running themes' will recur and it is important that you bear these in mind, mention them when appropriate and think about how they make an impact on the topic you are studying:

- *Transformational change* – change in form or ability.
- *Variational change* – the extent to which change varies from the agreed standard/norm.
- *Stage theory of development* – changes occur in stages which (according to Flavell, 1963) are qualitative, occur simultaneously with other behavioural changes and are rapid.
- *Dynamic systems approach* – a mathematical model is used to explain how qualitative changes result through small-scale quantitative changes, so it looks at how systems are affected by environmental change.

- **Connectionist approach** – is a computer-based modelling system in which there are many interconnected nodes at different levels and learning results from the strength of interaction between these.
- **Informational processing approach** – looks at the specific information processing that occurs in relation to individual tasks and how a child's ability changes over time.
- **Behaviourism** – the idea that all behaviours/characteristics are learnt either through the process of reinforcement or through vicarious learning (imitation).
- **Psychoanalytic viewpoint** – based on the work of Freud, this suggests that our behaviour is biologically determined by unconscious processes based on instincts; early experiences are seen as vitally important as it is believed they have a fundamental effect on later behaviour. Freud believed our personality develops in psychosexual stages with the most important development happening in childhood. The personality consists of three parts (the id, ego and superego) each of which has its own role, and disorder occurs when there are conflicts between them or when there are problems at early stages of development (the most common example is the Oedipal stage during which, Freud believed, a boy wishes to sleep with this mother but fears that if his father finds this out he will castrate him).
- **Cognitive developmental viewpoint** – refers to age-related changes that occur in mental activities such as learning and thinking.
- **Ethology** – studies the biological basis of behaviour including its evolution, causation and development (Cairns – 1979 in Shaffer (1993) p. 63).
- **Ethics** – a set of ethical guidelines must be followed which protect participants who take part in research projects. They include guidelines on consent, deception, debriefing, withdrawal from investigations, confidentiality and the protection of participants from psychological and physical harm.
- **Ecological validity** – the extent to which laboratory studies can be applied to the real world.
- **Nature** – behaviour is inborn/innate and due to evolution, genes and chemical make-up.
- **Nurture** – behaviour is due to the environment and learning experiences of the child.

These running themes will help you when using your textbooks as they underpin most topics in the syllabus and will show that there is common ground between these topics. When you are revising material these themes will also provide you with a way of linking your ideas together and building up a picture of how developmental psychology applies to the real world. As you will see throughout this book, such themes can be involved in a whole range of processes, for example in various types of development such as cognitive, motor and language. At the start of each section the themes most important to the topic are listed and in some cases expanded upon to give you some indication of the lines along which you could develop your thinking in relation to the material you will gain from your texts, and indeed from the sections themselves. Expanding upon these when writing your essays will ensure that you engage at a level of critical thinking that is vital if you want to gain the higher marks.

part two

course companion to the curriculum

2.1

research methods in developmental psychology

Core areas

- Case study
- Cohort effects
- Cross-sectional research
- Dependent variable
- Ethics
- Experimental method
- Experiments
- Independent variable
- Interviews
- Longitudinal research
- Matched pairs
- Observation
- Questionnaires
- Reliability
- Scientific method
- Validity

Learning outcomes

By the end of this section you should be able to:

- define the key research method terms;
- acknowledge the advantages and disadvantages of using these various methods to investigate child development;
- understand the ethical issues involved in researching children.

Running themes

- Ethics
- Transformational change
- Variational change

Introduction

Research with children can be conducted using a cross-sectional or longitudinal method.

Cross-sectional research is that which studies children of varying ages simultaneously. Cohort effects should be allowed for, since social change experienced by a group of varying ages may alter what is found.

Longitudinal research, on the other hand, studies data from each individual over a longer time period.

As in other areas of psychology, research in the developmental field should focus on the scientific method, that is, data analysis should be objective and in the pursuit of knowledge about child development. The section below covers the methods available when studying children and the pros and cons of using such methods.

Experiments

All experiments involve the manipulation of the independent variable (thing that is being changed) to see what effect it has on the dependent variable (thing that is being measured) while attempting to control the influence of other factors such as environment.

Laboratory	In the laboratory the researcher deliberately manipulates strict control over extraneous and confounding variables using standardised procedures.
Advantages	• An experimenter deliberately changes something to see if this does have an effect on something else. • As the laboratory environment is controlled, procedures can be standardised and therefore it is more likely that replication can occur, which is vital if the work is to be of scientific value. • Findings can be measured and recorded accurately as controlled environment.
Disadvantages	• Testing participants in laboratory conditions is unlike real-life situations (so this method can lack ecological validity) and participants may behave unnaturally unless deception is used, causing ethical problems. • Extraneous and confounding variables may still affect the study as total control is not possible.

Field	• The researcher deliberately manipulates the IV but does so in the participants' own natural environment.
Advantages	• Greater ecological validity as in participants' natural environment and therefore participant more likely to behave naturally. • Participant may not be aware of being tested, therefore less demand characteristics (behaving as they feel is expected).
Disadvantages	• If participants are not aware of being studied, issues of deception, consent, etc., arise. • As experimenter does not have full control over the environment, extraneous variables may affect the results and the study may be harder to replicate, which makes findings less valid.

Natural/Quasi	• The IV is changed by natural occurrence – the researcher just records the effect on the DV. Quasi-experiments are any in which control is lacking over the IV.
Advantages	• Greatest ecological validity as the experimenter is analysing something that has naturally occurred and the participants are therefore possibly unaware that they are part of a study.
Disadvantages	• May lead to ethical issues if participants not aware of being studied. • As a naturally occurring event it may be impossible to replicate or for the experimenter to have any control, therefore difficult to apply findings.

Many of the advantages and disadvantages of each type of experiment are simply reversed, so a laboratory-based study will offer control but is artificial, whereas a natural one is high in ecological validity but lacks control.

Experimental Design

Design	Advantages	Disadvantages
Repeated measures Same participants are used in each condition of the experiment.	Subject variables remain the same, as individual personality factors, etc., are same in both conditions. Less difficult for experimenter to find participants as can use same set in both conditions.	As participants take part in both conditions they are more likely to guess the aim of the study and therefore change behaviour (demand characteristics) or suffer order effects such as learning or boredom.
Independent groups Different participants are used in each condition of the experiment.	As participants only take part in one condition they are therefore less likely to guess the aim of the study and therefore change behaviour (demand characteristics) or suffer order effects such as learning or boredom.	As using different people in each condition it is possible that any differences found in the results are due to the varying characteristics of people in the two groups rather than anything else. Harder/more time-consuming for experimenter, who needs twice as many participants.
Matched pairs As above but participants are matched as closely as possible for any factors important for the study – so different but similar people are used.	Overcomes difficulties of independent groups as experimenter does try to match participants, so subject variables are more constant, but still decreases chances of demand characteristics.	Not frequently used, as locating a matched sample is time-consuming and difficult. It is very difficult to match participants in every possible way.

REMEMBER

Experiments

> In the laboratory the researcher deliberately manipulates strict control over extraneous and confounding variables using standardised procedures.
> In field experiments the researcher deliberately manipulates the IV but does so in the participant's own natural environment.
> With natural experiments the IV is changed by natural occurrence – the researcher just records the effect on the DV. Quasi-experiments are any in which control over the IV is lacking.
> Repeated measures – the same participants are used in each condition of the experiment.
> Independent groups – different participants are used in each condition of the experiment.
> Matched pairs – as above but participants are matched as closely as possible for any factors important for the study – so different but similar people are used.

Observation

Looks at the behaviour of participants in various situations and is 'a relatively unconstrained segment of a person's freely chosen behaviour as it occurs' (Coolican, 1990).

Observation	Advantages	Disadvantages
Structured Structured so that observers classify behaviour in set ways.	As all observers know what they are coding, should lead to increased inter-rater reliability.	May miss important information as only set behaviours are observed and therefore lacks ecological validity.
	Less researcher bias as observation is structured and clearly operationalised/defined.	Leads to demand characteristics if participants are aware of being studied.

Naturalistic Observes people in their natural environment.	Richer data obtained, and as studied in natural setting has higher ecological validity. Less influence from experimenter effects. More ethical, as natural behaviour.	Researcher may gain such a variety of information that analysis is difficult. Inter-rater reliability may be harder to achieve due to the high number of variables that may be observed, and therefore less validity. Ethical issues if observer does not disclose purpose or gain consent.
Participant Observes participants in their natural environment but observes and participates in the group being studied.	High ecological validity as researcher truly experiences the situation.	Ethical issues as above. Subject to experimenter effects as researcher will find it harder to remain unbiased if a participant in the situation.

Handy Hint! Data collection

Can be done using notes, tape recordings, video recordings or one-way mirrors. These methods vary in their usefulness because, for example, notes are easy but other important information may be missed while writing. On the other hand, videos give all the information required but can be intrusive and may change participants' behaviour.

Handy Hint! Sampling methods

Methods include time sampling (behaviour is observed for a set period of time), event sampling (every time the behaviour occurs a note is made) or point sampling (the behaviour of just a given individual or group is noted at a time). These are useful in providing accurate observations but may miss important information.

Handy Hint! Classifying data

Data is usually classified using frequency grids/tally charts, rating scales or timings of behaviour.

Problems of Observation

Issues of Disclosure – there are ethical issues involved in studying people without their consent. *But* if people are aware that they are being studied they may behave differently, leading to social desirability bias and demand characteristics.

Observer Bias – especially experimenter/observer expectancy where each observer differs in the way they perceive, value and label behaviour, which results in a bias.

Inter-rater Reliability – there is a need to compare observations between researchers to ensure they are reliable.

Case studies

Common in developmental psychology, these involve the detailed study and data collection of one individual.

Handy Hints! Advantages and disadvantages of case studies

They give unique insight into individual histories and into certain areas, which may not be gained when collecting data across a group of individuals. As such, case studies have high ecological validity. The difficulty comes, however, with generalising findings from an individual more widely, and here reliability and validity can be questionable not least because the researcher-participant relationship is often closer than would be the case for other research methods.

Questionnaires

A questionnaire uses various types of questions to make a quick and efficient assessment of people's attitudes. It may contain the following question types:

Fixed choice/closed-ended Questions

These are questions for which limited answers are available, for example, 'yes'/'no', or on a scale from 'strongly disagree' to 'strongly agree' (a Likert scale).

advantages – answers are quantifiable, which means each answer can be added up to give a total which indicates the strength of an attitude in one direction or the other.

disadvantages – by allowing participants a fixed response one is forcing them to give an answer they might not otherwise give and does not allow them to elaborate.

Open-ended Questions

These allow participants to contribute their own views to a question where a number of answers may be given.

advantages – these questions allow researchers to collect information they may not have thought about and this type of questionnaire gives a rich and comprehensive picture of people's feelings and opinions on the topic being investigated.

disadvantages – the information given may be difficult to summarise and quantify, and coding of categories may later have to be used.

REMEMBER

It is vitally important when using questionnaires to ensure they are *reliable* (consistent in what they are measuring) and *valid* (measuring what they intend to). To ensure this, test–retest can be used. This is where the same group is tested over two different periods to ensure similar responses are collated. Piloting the questionnaire can ensure validity.

The following types of questions should be avoided	These are a problem because
Double-barrelled questions	The participant is being asked two different questions at once.
Leading questions	They lead people into giving the socially desirable answer.
Factual questions (question containing a fact)	If a fact is given it is difficult for participants to disagree with the statement but they may not actually indicate that they agree with it.
Ambiguous questions	People may not give a true response if they are unclear about what a question means.
Complex questions	If questions are too long with too many concepts or too much technical language, participants may misunderstand and therefore not give a true reflection of their views.
Emotive questions	They rely on emotional appeal and may encourage participants to give an answer that reflects their emotion at the time, or may lead to social desirability bias

Advantages and disadvantages of questionnaires

Advantages	Disadvantages
• Can use a standardised procedure therefore ensuring reliable results. • Allows similar treatment of all participants.	• Only simple responses available. • Does not allow expansion of information. • Artificial questioning process and misinterpretation of questions possible.

• Get less bias from interpersonal factors, as not testing on a one-to-one basis but on paper/group. • Quick and easy to administer. • Useful for gathering data from large numbers of participants. • Easy to replicate and score.	• May produce distorted answers. • Risk of social desirability bias. • May get low return rate. • Need good sampling to be of general use.

Interviews

Interviews are similar to questionnaires but are conducted verbally. Qualitative data may be collected (giving responses which can be statistically classified) or quantitative (descriptive in nature).

Interviews range from being informal through to being fully structured, as detailed below.

Informal/non-directive

- Overall aim is to gather data.
- The person can talk about anything they choose.
- The psychologist has no influence on the topics the person wishes to discuss but may help and guide the discussion in order to increase the individual's self-awareness.

Informal but guided

The interview is informal but the interviewer may have a list of topics that could be covered in the interview.

Clinical interviews

Frequently used in developmental psychology, these are semi-structured, so account for the individual while testing a general assumption/hypothesis.

Structured but open-ended

- Use a standardised procedure in which the interviewer asks pre-set questions.
- The interviewee can still express how they feel if they are given open-ended questions.

Fully structured

- Here the interview follows a fixed format.
- The questions are often closed-ended – that is they have a fixed response.

REMEMBER

The advantages of the informal versus the structured interview are provided below.

	Informal	**Structured**
Advantages	• Interview is flexible and can be suited to the individual responses, situation, context and needs of participants. • As such, results have high validity as the person is likely to feel more relaxed and give natural responses. • Participant does not have to give a fixed response and therefore vast and full information is obtained.	• Method is quick to conduct as it asks the same questions each time, and is therefore standardised and can be used by a number of researchers simultaneously. • As data is structured, it is easy to analyse. • Researcher can ensure that all relevant topic areas are covered and there is less opportunity for experimenter effects because of the structured nature of the interview.

		• Is easy to replicate as fixed data are obtained.
Disadvantages	• Data gathered is unsystematic and because it varies between individuals it may subsequently be hard to analyse. • The techniques may be subject to experimenter effects, demand characteristics and social desirability bias where the researcher influences the responses given or participant gives those they feel are expected.	• Data has less validity as it is not tailored to the needs of individuals and only offers fixed responses. • A structured interview has less ecological validity as participants are not necessarily able to offer natural responses. • Information gathered is too narrow and therefore method has low validity.

Relationship between researcher and participants

In psychology a number of factors can influence the relationship between researchers and participants. For example, the participants may guess the aim of the research and try to act accordingly or show social desirability bias. It is also possible that researchers may conduct their work in such a way that they convey their expectations to participants.

Demand characteristics

This is where the participant works out the aim of the study and therefore behaves differently (either to please the experimenter or to spoil the study).

Avoid by:

- *Using independent measures designed to stop exposure to both conditions of the study, thereby reducing the chances of guessing the aim of the study.*
- *Using deception could be used to hide the research aim but this would result in ethical problems.*
- *Using a single blind technique – here the participant does not know which condition of the study they are in.*

Social desirability bias

This is where the participant tries to 'look good' or respond in a socially desirable way.

Avoid by:

- *Using a design by which people are unaware of being observed/researched – but this can result in ethical problems.*
- *Including 'lie scales', such that participants who are not being truthful can be identified and excluded from the analyses.*

Experimenter expectancy (a type of investigator effect)

This is where the expectations of the researcher influence the results by either consciously or unconsciously revealing the desired outcome through procedural or recording bias.

Avoid by:

- *Using a double-blind technique by which neither the participant nor the researcher carrying out the procedure/recording the results knows the hypothesis or which condition participants are in.*
- *Using inter-rater reliability to compare the ratings from the various observers to see if they are similar and thus reliable.*

Reliability and validity are also important when collecting data in developmental psychology.

Reliability

A test is reliable if it measures a variable consistently.

internal reliability – refers to how consistent a method measures within itself (if it measures one thing consistently), a process helped by standardisation (using the same process with each participant).

Test this – *by the split-half method in which a test (e.g., on stress) is split in half and the scores on each half are then calculated. If the results indicate consistency (and correlate) it is assumed that the test is reliable.*

external reliability – tests the reliability of a method over time.

Test this – *by the test/re-test method by which (as it sounds) you carry out the test on more than one occasion (with the same participant) and if scores are consistent (and correlate) then it is assumed to be reliable.*

Validity

A test is valid if it measures what it is supposed to and if variables are therefore operationalised (clearly defined so that they are measurable).

face/content validity – on the face of it, does the content of the test look like it measures what it claims to?

ecological validity – can the method be applied to real-life situations and therefore does it measure naturally occurring behaviour?

predictive validity – can a test accurately predict future performance (e.g., good GCSE scores indicate good AS results)?

concurrent validity – if the test replicates established data and results correlate then it must be valid.

construct validity – the test must support the underlying constructs it is measuring (e.g., if a person has high blood pressure induced by anxiety then an anxiety questionnaire should support this).

Ethics

There are a number of ethical issues, as detailed below, that psychologists should bear in mind when studying children. Principally, the guidelines issued by the Society for Research in Child Development (SRCD) must be followed.

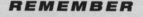

REMEMBER

These emphasise the importance of obtaining consent and the procedures that can be employed, stressing that no harm (psychological or physiological) be caused and stress-free procedures be employed if possible.

Additional general guidelines (Published by the British Psychological Society) should be followed. These include those relating to the areas below:

confidentiality – participants must be assured that all information gained during investigations will be kept confidential as required by the Data Protection Act and that publication of any findings subsequently will not allow them to be identified.

debriefing – while debriefing does not justify unethical practices, it is used to further the participants' understanding of the aims and processes of the research in which they have taken part. This is to ensure that they do not later suffer any psychological harm from their participation and allows them to gain a full understanding of what and why procedures have been used and what results were then obtained.

deception – it is unethical to deceive/mislead/withhold information from participants, knowingly or unknowingly, about the aims or procedures of any research, unless there is strong scientific justification agreed by an ethics committee.

ethical guidelines – these are sets of guidelines which protect participants who take part in research projects. They include guidelines on consent, deception, debriefing, and withdrawal from investigations, confidentiality and the protection of participants from psychological and physical harm.

informed consent – all participants are required to give consent to take part in scientific research (or, in the case of children or other vulnerable groups, consent must be given on their behalf) and this entails informing them of the demands, objectives and possible effects of the study. It is believed that only after gaining such information can a participant make an informed decision concerning their willingness to participate.

protection of participants from harm – during the course of research participants should not be subject to any risk of harm beyond what they would normally expect from their lifestyle. Psychologists must prioritise the safety and physical/psychological well-being of their participants above all else.

withdrawal from investigations – before commencing any research the investigator must assure participants that they may leave the study at any time should they wish to do so, and there is a duty to ensure that the environment permits this. Withdrawal is permitted even if participants have volunteered, or been paid to participate and even if they have completed a study but then wish their data to be disregarded.

Tasks

1 Using the research projects outlined below, identify whether a longitudinal or cross-sectional study was being carried out. Explain your answer.

   (a) A group of children aged between 18 months and 3 years, who have spent their lives in an orphanage, are studied at ages 7, 10 and 16 to assess their social and emotional development.
   (b) Children's ability to read and write is examined across a group of nursery and foundation stage children.
   (c) Ability to recognise gender stereotypical roles in a videotape of various professions (e.g. policeman) is assessed in a group of children aged 7–10 years old.

(d)   The effects of day care are examined in children who spent their first three years in nursery care and their cognitive and emotional skills are measured at ages 7, 11, 16 and 18.

2 Using your textbooks, research one psychological study that employs each of the following research methods and describe in a few lines how the study was carried out: an observation, an interview, a questionnaire, an experiment, a case study.

3 For each of these examples identify the advantages and disadvantages of using this type of method to research children in each of the individual pieces of research.

Essay questions

"Outline and evaluate the research methods employed by developmental psychologists"

This question requires two skills. It is not asking you to simply list all the research methods available but is asking you to look at the wide of range of methods in a critical light – assessing their usefulness in developmental psychology. In other words, you also need to discuss their advantages and disadvantages not just as a list but in relation to specific developmental issues, referring wherever possible to relevant studies. This shows the examiner that you can apply what you are being taught rather than simply learning and regurgitating material. Since there are numerous methods available it may also help you to be selective and focus on those you consider most applicable to the developmental field, and ones you can support by wider research. If this is the way you are planning to go, make sure you are specific in outlining those areas you will focus on, in the introductory section of your essay.

"Consider the special ethical issues involved in developmental psychology"

To start this essay it will help to give a general outline of the ethical principles underpinning psychological research as proposed by the BPS. You will then need to become more specific and highlight the areas that are more pertinent to the developmental field, and the special areas that need to be considered. If you were to simply write a list it would not be sufficient to constitute an essay. Again, you need to locate this within the research context, discussing and supporting the ethical issues with practical examples from this area of psychology.

Common Pitfalls

- *If you are not familiar with the research methods used in psychology it would be all too easy to concentrate purely on learning the material in this section and hence focus exclusively on the research methods but not in relation to studying children – remember this is your developmental psychology unit and this is therefore what the examiner will be looking for.*
- *As in all areas of this unit you need to think critically about the material you wish to discuss. Simply knowing the types of methods that can be used is not enough. It is also critical that you look at the advantages and disadvantages of the methods used.*
- *Similarly, knowing the ethical guidelines appropriate to studying children is critical. While many of the general ones quoted by the BPS apply, you need to relate them specifically to the use of children. For example, consent must be obtained but saying this is not alone sufficient since children would not necessarily be capable of doing so. You therefore need to make it clear that an appropriate adult may do this on their behalf. Do not therefore forget to consider the special ethical issues involved with children.*

Textbook Guide

BERK, L. E. (2005). *Child development* (7th ed.) Pearson International Edition. Chapter 2 on research strategies is useful as it includes material on common methods when studying children, reliability and validity, general research decisions and ethics.

COOLICAN, H. (2004). *Research methods and statistics in psychology* (4th ed.) London: Hodder & Stoughton. Provides a very simple and straightforward account of the various types of research methods that can be used in psychology.

TETI, D. M. (ED.) (2004). *The handbook of research methods in developmental science.* Blackwell Publishing. This covers a collection of newly written articles that provide an overview of methods and approaches associated with the study of human development.

www.srcd.org. Website detailing the guidelines for the ethical treatment of children in research.

2.2

perceptual development

Core areas

- Behavioural methods
- Differentiation theory
- Enrichment theory
- Eye movements
- Habituation
- Interactionist view
- Perceptual adaptation
- Perceptual adjustment
- Perceptual deprivation
- Physiology
- Preference methods
- Shape constancy
- Size constancy
- Stimulus seeking
- Visual cliff
- Visual preference tasks
- Visual reinforcement

Learning outcomes

By the end of this section you should be able to:

- define key terms;
- acknowledge the work of key thinkers in this area and evaluate their studies/ theories;
- provide an overview of the developmental sequences children show in terms of perception;
- understand the relevance of the nature–nurture debate in relation to perceptual development.

Running themes

- Cognitive-developmental approach
- Ecological validity
- Ethics
- Nature
- Nurture
- Transformational change
- Variational change

Introduction

D.R. Shaffer (1993: 222) provides a comprehensive definition of what we can consider perceptual development the study of. He says:

> perhaps we can agree that perceptual development is the growth of interpretive skills – a complex process that depends, in part, on the expression of individual genotypes, the maturation of the sensory receptors, the kinds of sensory experiences that the child has available to analyse and interpret, the child's emerging cognitive abilities, and the social context in which all these other variables operate.

Development as a whole is a complex process and perception is just one area which may impact on various other areas.

Shaffer (1993) outlined three stages in the development of perception in the first year of life:

- **0–2** months is the stimulus-seeking stage where babies discriminate between visual stimuli
- **2–6** months is the form-constructing stage where form and shape are perceived
- **6–12** months leads to form-interpretation where infants start to make sense of what they see.

The nature–nurture debate is an important one in perceptual development and there is evidence for both views, as seen throughout this section. Essentially, developmental theories argue that perception is an innate ability, while those on perceptual adaptation and readjustment studies suggest it is a result of learning. For example, animal studies such as that carried out by Blakemore and Cooper (1970) indicated that kittens exposed to only vertical and horizontal lines in their environment only developed physiological pathways resembling this perceptual orientation and could only respond to this.

Obviously caution must be applied when transferring such an assumption to humans, although research into adaptation shows some evidence for both a mixture of learning and inborn ability.

Methods used to study perceptual development include:

- *Behavioural methods* – examine if behaviour changes in response to what is being perceived, e.g., whether children will react to a room that appears to have moving walls and ceiling (see Butterworth & Cicchetti, 1978).
- *Preference methods* – a child's preference for one stimulus over another is simply observed (the longer the looking time suggests a preference for that stimulus).
- *Habituation* – something is presented and the time spent looking at it before moving on to something else is measured (that is, until the infant has shown habituation). If he has moved on to a second stimulus it indicates perception has taken place as he has shown discrimination between the two.
- *Eye movement* – eye movements are tracked.
- *Physiology* – brain-wave activity (visual evoked potentials) or other indirect physiological responses to a stimulus, such as heart rate can be measured.
- *Visual reinforcement* – when the response to a stimulus is evident then it remains but when the attention decreases it is changed. The idea is that visual response is reinforced in some way by a device the child has control of and can be altered when more reinforcement is needed.

REMEMBER

Methods of studying perceptual development

Various methods can be used, including looking at behaviour, preferences, habituation, eye-movements, physiology and reinforcement.

Key thinkers/theories

Fantz (1961) – perceptual development – visual preference task

Young infants (4 days–5 months) were shown discs that were either blank or with features that resembled human facial features in the correct position or jumbled up, and showed a preference for ones most closely resembling a face. He believed this supported the view that perception was innate and that a preference for social stimuli was developed at even a basic level at this age.

Gibson and Walk (1960) – perceptual development – the visual cliff

A 'visual cliff', which was actually a table-top with glass, was designed whereby a check pattern was placed under one side (shallow end) and on the floor beneath the top on the other (deep end). Results found that babies (6.5–12 months) were reluctant to crawl on to the deep side, thus supporting the idea that depth cues are innate because they are developed even at this age.

Piaget (1952) – perceptual development – enrichment theory

Originally infants develop their sensory and motor abilities in the sensori-motor stage occurring before the age of two and interaction with the world aids the development of innate schemas, after which new ones can be formed through the process of accommodation. Perception therefore occurs because it is influenced by the expectations that result from such schemas.

Differentiation theory – perceptual development

Perception develops once distinctive features of objects can be trans-ferred across situations and once they can be differentiated from irrele-vant stimuli. Such differentiation tends to occur as a result of age.

Handy Hints for evaluating the work of key thinkers/theories

- It hard to generalise the results from Fantz's work as it contained a very small sample size and one cannot be sure that the preference was due to the human resemblance rather than the overall symmetrical pattern.
- It is possible that failure to climb on to the deep side of Gibson and Walk's 'visual cliff' was a result of environmental learning/experience.
- It is hard to isolate the development of perception from other cognitive processes using Piaget's theory because it was intended as a whole theory of cognitive development, and to focus on just one aspect of it is inaccurate.

Stages of perceptual development

Early pattern recognition is found as early as 0–2 months as indicated in Fantz's work outlined above. This is the stimulus-seeking stage because the infant simply has a biological urge to scan the environment and explore any stimuli she can see well. It becomes more systematic over time and the process enhances further biological maturation of the visual areas of the brain.

Later pattern and form recognition develop between 2 months and 1 year, where discrimination between objects, and from their background, is now possible. There is some suggestion that perception of movement is also possible at this stage. Shape constancy (where an object is seen as the same shape despite orientation) appears to develop at about 3 months, as Caron et al. (1979) discovered when using the habituation technique. In Infants 75–85 days old, Bower (1966) found some evidence for size constancy.

Social perception becomes established as the first six months of life sees recognition of familiar people, and in the next six months this develops so that emotional expression can be interpreted and can be used to regulate behaviour (social referencing). Construction and interpretation of form also improves.

REMEMBER

Stages of perceptual development

➢ Neonates – can see patterns, colours and detect changes in brightness.
➢ First 2 months – sees them acting as 'stimulus seekers' where they prefer complex, moving, high-contrast stimuli.
➢ 3–6 months – forms and familiar faces are recognised. Spatial awareness starts to develop, particularly reactions to approaching objects, size constancy and depth cues.
➢ 6 months plus – sees increasing perceptual development of wide-ranging aspects such as recognition, size, depth and distance.

Nature vs nurture

While some research into the perceptual development of neonates points towards an innate element, this cannot be the whole story since we would otherwise all possess the same abilities regardless of experience and this is not the case. It would therefore seem that the environment also influences the development of perception in a number of different ways. Deprivation studies indicate that normal development is at least partially dependent on exposure to various/patterned stimuli.

Studies to support this include the work of Reisen (1950) who raised chimps in the dark and then found that they were unable to distinguish patterns. That of Held and Hein (1963) also highlights this issue. Here kittens were raised in the dark until they were 8–12 weeks old and then assigned to an active, or passive, condition which basically either enabled them to physically move within and interact in their environment, or not. The effect on perception was marked, as those who had been placed in the passive condition showed little awareness of depth, thus suggesting that movement is an important environmental factor in some aspects of perceptual development.

> *Be aware that caution should be applied when generalising the findings of animal experiments to humans. You might also want to consider the ethical issues of such work.*

Conclusion

The interactionist view holds that perception is a bit of both nature and nurture. The environment is important as it aids the development of the visual equipment we are born with, for example by triggering neurological responses and thus contributing to the development of the brain, sensory receptors and linking neural pathways. Most critically the experiences of the child will contribute to the interpretations that can be made of the visual world. For example, expectation about what may be seen is influenced by the early experiences of the child, and also by the basic layout of objects in the world – thus a cultural element is introduced.

Tasks

1 Look back to the techniques employed to study perceptual development. Using your textbooks research a study that uses each of these and for each one write a paragraph on how that method was carried out.

2 Using the overview provided in this section and the more detailed information in your books, compile a timeline to represent perceptual development in the early years.

3 Divide an A4 piece of paper lengthwise in half. On one side head the column 'nature' and on the other 'nurture'. Underneath the appropriate section now list the evidence that can be used to support the idea that perception is either something that is innate, or due to experience. Now expand upon why the work you list supports this view. This will provide an essay plan for one of the titles outlined below.

Essay questions

"What do research studies tell us about the development of perception?"

Notice the focus here is on research studies. In any opening paragraph you may want to highlight the nature–nurture debate and its relevance to perceptual development. You then have opposing research studies to highlight the aspects of this debate. Fantz's study will need to be outlined in detail and then you should show what this research actually tells us about perceptual development, that is, it highlights that it is an innate skill. This can then be balanced out by Gibson and Walk's study on the visual cliff; again, you will need to outline this before expanding on how it supports the idea that perception is a result of learning. Since neither study alone can account for each view, the notes of caution should be discussed, all the time referring back to what these points say about perceptual development.

"Discuss the nature–nurture debate as it applies to perception"

This is a critical area within this topic and you need to be very clear in advance about what evidence tends towards perception being innate, and which tends towards it being a result of experience. Since the essay does not simply require a list but needs you to expand upon why the research you have covered supports the given argument, you should not only report the study but go on to reflect your understanding of its relevance. Some evidence for nature comes, for example, from Fantz's work, that of Gibson and Walk and from the stages of early development. However nurture is evident from the research on readjustment and from animal studies. Notes of caution about the ecological validity and ethics of such work can be mentioned before drawing an overall conclusion which should reflect the interactionist viewpoint that innate abilities are developed as a result of interaction with the environment/experience.

Common Pitfalls

- Undoubtedly perceptual development is an extensive topic with many difficult terms to grasp, and students frequently mix these up. It may therefore be useful to draw up a list of definitions to revise at the start of this topic.
- When studying perceptual development ensure that you can relate the data back to a discussion on nature–nurture, and therefore prepare, in advance, how each study supports a nature, or nurture, argument.
- The stages of development in perception often consist of many simultaneous changes in different areas, for example, size, shape, and depth. Ensure you have a good grasp of what development occurs when (and to what extent).
- Don't forget to evaluate the studies, including the validity and ethics involved in this area.

Textbook Guide

BRUCE, V., GREEN, P. R., & GEORGESON, M. A. (1966). *Visual perception: physiology, psychology and ecology.* Hove UK. This provides a more detailed coverage of those topics involved in perception.

FANTZ, R. L. (1961). The origin of form perception. *Scientific American, 204,* 66–72. Original coverage of this important study.

GIBSON, E. J., & WALK, R. D. (1960). The visual cliff. *Scientific American, 202,* 64–71. Original coverage of this important study.

2.3	
cognitive development	

Core areas

- Accommodation
- Animistic thinking
- Assimilation
- Centration
- Compensation
- Concrete operation
- Conservation
- Class inclusion tasks
- Classification
- Disequilibrium
- Egocentrism
- Enactive stage
- Equilibrium
- Formal operation
- General symbolic function
- Iconic stage
- Information processing approach

- Internalisation
- Intuitive stage
- Object permanence
- Operations
- Pre-conceptual stage
- Pre-operational stage
- Primary circular reactions
- Reversibility
- Scaffolding
- Schemata
- Secondary circular reactions
- Sensorimotor stage
- Seriation
- Symbolic mode
- Syncretic reasoning
- Theory of mind
- Transductive reasoning
- Zone of proximal development

Learning outcomes

By the end of this section you should be able to:

- define the key terms outlined above and understand in which cognitive theory they belong;
- acknowledge and describe each of the theories on cognitive development including those of Piaget, Bruner, Vygotsky, theory of mind and the information processing approach;
- evaluate the theories using research studies such as the Swiss mountain experiment and false belief tasks, for example;
- discuss the weaknesses of the theories and how they can be compared and contrasted.

Running themes

- Cognitive developmental viewpoint
- Ecological validity
- Ethics
- Informational processing approach
- Nature
- Nurture
- Stage theory of development
- Transformational change

Introduction

Cognitive development refers to the development of a child's thinking, problem-solving and linguistic abilities. It is therefore an important area in developmental psychology and one which covers a range of different theories including those of Piaget, Bruner, Vygotsky, the information processing approach and theory of mind.

Key thinkers in cognitive development

Piaget (1967)

> *Piaget believes that the child adapts to its environment and constructs its own understanding of the world. Thus intelligence is a process which changes over time.*

The basic unit of intelligence is a *schema*, which is an internal representation of a specific physical or mental action. Schemas change through a process of assimilation and accommodation. *Assimilation* is where the child fits the world into existing schemas and *accommodation* involves changing existing schemas to fit the world. This is important as it allows the child to change schemas to match the requirements of the environment which then brings about a state of equilibrium. Most critically, Piaget said that there are four stages of development:

Sensorimotor stage (0–2 years) – the child experiences the world (mainly) through its immediate perceptual and physical (sensory and motor) abilities. *Primary circular reactions* emerge at 1–4 months, where basic reflex or motor movements are made as a function of one's own body. However, by 4–8 months the infant's attention is focused on objects outside of the body (*secondary circular reactions*). At 8–12 months the child combines previously acquired schemata, and then trial and error methods are employed to learn about properties of objects by 12–18 months. Mental combination becomes possible by the end of this stage. *Object permanence* is where a baby understands that objects continue to exist even when they are not being perceived or manipulated in some way. A lack of object permanence is usually evident at the beginning of this stage and reflects *egocentrism*, where the baby can only see the world from its own perspective and thinks that people see the world in the same way as it does, thus failing to distinguish between itself and the rest of the world. This stage is also important for the development of the *general symbolic function*, that is, the use of mental images, words and other symbols to represent the world.

Pre-operational stage (2–7 years) – in this stage the child is still largely influenced by the way objects look/how they seem, rather than by any particular logic. Piaget says that pre-operational children can do some things they were unable to do before 2 years, and that they engage in deferred imitation, symbolic play, drawing, mental imagery and use of language, all of which have a semiotic (symbolic) function. However, some operations still pose problems because the child continues to have an egocentric perspective and uses *syncretic reasoning* by linking neighbouring objects or events together on the basis of common elements. In the **pre-conceptual stage (2–4 years)** the child's thinking makes it difficult for it to understand relative terms, for example, 'bigger' rather than big or biggest. The child can only classify things on the basis of a single attribute (*centration*) and has difficulty with *seriation*, that is, the arrangement of objects on the basis of a particular dimension. He draws incorrect inferences about the relationship between two objects based on a single attribute (*transductive reasoning*), which leads to *animistic thinking*, that is, the belief that inanimate objects are alive. During the **intuitive stage (4–7 years)** the ability to think logically is still limited and on *class inclusion tasks* the child fails to understand the relationship between superordinate and subordinate classes. Piaget and Inhelder have also shown in their Swiss mountain experiment (1956) that children remain self-centred and egocentric since it has been shown that they cannot put themselves 'in someone else's shoes'. Another feature of the pre-operational stage is the child's *inability to conserve*, where the child fails to understand that things remain the same (constant) despite changes in appearance (how they look). Studies on the conservation of liquid, number, quantity and weight indicate this – for example, a child will fail to perceive that a tall thin beaker contains the same amount of liquid as a short fat one. These studies of conservation show that the pre-operational child believes that things are as they look; the child demonstrates identity but not *compensation* and *reversibility* (the ability to work backwards mentally), all of which are necessary for conservation.

Concrete-operational stagfe (7–11 years) – the main features of this stage are the acquisition of *reversible thinking, the ability to centre*, *classification* and *seriation*. Thus the child is able to think backwards mentally and is less egocentric and capable of grouping objects together logically in terms of their common characteristics, as well as being able to arrange items in rank order in terms of colour or size (for example). Transivity tasks still remain a problem but here the child starts to manipulate and experiment with real objects in order to solve problems in a logical way.

Formal-operational stage (11–15 years) – here the individual shows an ability to reason in the abstract without having to rely on concrete objects/events, and the child's thinking resembles that of an adult. The child is able to solve a problem in its head by systematically testing out several propositions, by isolating such propositions and at the same time considering their interrelatedness.

Bruner (Bruner et al., 1966)

Bruner was influenced by Piaget and also believed that children are born with a biological organisation that helps them understand their world, and that their underlying cognitive structure matures over time so that they can think about their world in an increasingly complex way. However, rather than looking at stages of development Bruner emphasised modes of representing the world and focused on three particular ways: **Enactive (0–1 year)** – at first babies represent the world through actions, any knowledge being based upon what they have experienced through their own behaviour. Past events are represented through appropriate motor responses and in repeated encounters with the environment automatic patterns emerge. The **iconic stage (1–6 years)** is concerned with images, and this form of representation involves building up a mental image of things we have experienced and such images are usually made up of past encounters with similar objects or situations. Bruner's main interest was in the transition between the iconic and **symbolic modes** at about **6/7 years**.

> For Bruner language was seen as being crucial and language and thought seen as inseparable, because he felt that without language human thought would be limited only to what could be learnt through actions or images.

Vygotsky (1962)

He believed that social interaction and language were the main factors in cognitive development, because participation in social activity, he felt, developed the individual's capabilities. Cognitive development involves an active internalisation of the problem-solving processes that take place between people (child–adult) and the child receives guidance, knowledge and skills from those who already possess them. He used the term *scaffolding* to describe the support/context the adult provides for the child. Therefore development changes as the meaning of social interaction is internalised.

Internalisation of language is seen as the main area of development and occurs in three stages: pre-intellectual social speech (0–3 years) where thinking and language are not contingent, egocentric speech (3–7 years) where language is used aloud and alongside behaviour and inner speech (7+) where the child uses speech silently to control their own behaviour but also publicly for social communication. The *zone of proximal development* defines those functions that have not yet matured but are in the process of maturation. The actual developmental level characterises mental development retrospectively and the zone of proximal development characterises mental development prospectively.

REMEMBER

Key Thinkers: Piaget

> Piaget believed that the basic unit of intelligence is a schema which is an internal representation of a specific physical or mental action, and schemas change through a process of assimilation and accommodation.

> In the sensorimotor stage (0–2 years) the child experiences the world (mainly) through its immediate perceptual and physical (sensory and motor) ability. Object permanence, egocentrism and the development of the general symbolic function are important in this stage.

> In the pre-operational stage the child is still largely influenced by the way objects look/how they seem rather than by any particular logic. The child can only classify things on the basis of a single attribute (centration) and has difficulty with seriation, that is, the arrangement of objects on the basis of a particular dimension. He draws incorrect inferences about the relationship between two objects based on a single attribute (transductive reasoning) which leads to animistic thinking (the belief that inanimate objects are alive). The ability to think logically is still limited and on class-inclusion tasks the child fails to understand the relationship between superordinate and subordinate classes. The child is unable to conserve, whereby it fails to understand that things remain the same (constant) despite changes in appearance (how they look).

> The main features of the concrete-operational stage are the acquisition of reversible thinking, the ability to centre, classification and seriation.

> In the formal-operational stage the individual shows an ability to reason in the abstract without having to rely on concrete objects/events and the child's thinking resembles that of an adult.

Handy Hints for evaluating the work of key thinkers in cognitive development

- Bruner et al. (1966) supported Bruner's work. Children from 4–7 years old were given the orthodox Piagetian task (pre-test) and almost all of the 4–5-year-olds said that there was more liquid in the taller, thinner beaker as did about half of the 6–7-year-olds. The children were then shown two standard beakers and a third, wider beaker. All three were screened – so when the contents of the standard ones were poured into the wider one, children could not see the level of the liquid, but only the tops of the beakers. They were then asked which had the most liquid, with the screen still covering the liquid level.

Most 5–7-year-olds answered correctly that it was the same, as did about half of the 4-year-olds. When the screen was removed, all 4-year-olds reverted to their pre-screening answer but all the others stuck to the answers given while the screen was in place. Finally, in the post-test situation two standard beakers and a taller, thinner one were used (without a screen); the 4-year-olds were unaffected by having seen the beakers screened, although the success rate of the 5–7-year-olds rose. Such results supported Bruner, because they showed that when a child's speech was activated by having them 'say' their judgement when the screen was covering the liquid levels (symbolic mode) it prevented iconic mode domination, although this could only be applied once cognitive maturation occurred at approximately 5 years.

- Support for Piaget's idea that the child is incapable of visual perspective-taking comes from Piaget and Inhelder's Swiss mountain experiment (1956). They used a 3D model of a mountain scene with three mountains with snow on top. The child explores the model and then sits on one side while a doll is placed on the other. The child is then asked what the doll can see, and is shown a set of ten pictures taken from different angles and asked to point out the answer. Piaget found that the child was only able to choose a photo which matched how they themselves saw the model, supporting the idea of egocentrism.

- Piaget's work has been criticised for many reasons. For example some believe that a linguistic explanation can be offered rather than failure being because of a lack of logical competence. So, the child fails to understand questions containing words like 'more' or 'less' due to a linguistic incompetence that means the questions cannot be fully comprehended, rather than a reasoning inability. It has also been argued that pre-operational children fail on concrete operational tasks, not because of knowledge but because the researcher gives misleading cues. Similarly, with regards to experimental validity, Piagetian tasks are abstract and artificial and therefore failure could be due to lack of familiarity to the child and everyday life. Research has shown that cognitive competence is displayed if the tasks are recognisable ones.

Information Processing Approach (IPA)

According to this approach, the human mind is like a computer, or an information processing system capable of the input, storage, retrieval and output of information. Three stages are involved: input from an external stimulus or problem, followed by a decision about the application of the appropriate system for this problem, and lastly the output response or action. Such processes are automatic, and as the brain matures information is transferred to neurons faster and so processing speed increases as a result of such maturation, but also because of experience, for example in the organisation of information.

The information processing approach emphasises the detailed analysis of the processing involved in individual tasks and how such tasks are modelled in computer programming.

Theory/understanding of mind

Theory of mind is concerned with the way we assess and theorise about the mental states of others and is usually tested using false belief tasks. Here a child is given a scenario and is judged according to whether or not it will apply a knowingly incorrect decision itself, or show awareness of another acting 'incorrectly'. The most famous of these tests is the Sally–Anne test (Baron-Cohen, Leslie, & Frith, 1985). Here the experimenter usually sits opposite a child with two dolls – Sally and Anne. Sally puts a marble in a basket and leaves and then Anne comes along, takes the marble and hides it in her own box. Sally then returns. The child is then asked to identify where Sally will look for her marble. If they say Sally's basket then it shows they have an understanding of mind because they can represent the doll's false belief. Indicating Anne's basket, however, shows a failure to account for Sally's false belief. Results indicate that most 3-year-olds fail this task but 4–5-year-olds pass it. There is a wealth of research into autistic children in this area which is beyond the scope of this section. However, in brief, autistic children appear to find this scenario extremely difficult and it has therefore been argued that one of the key features of autism is a lack of understanding of mind.

Note that although this work tells us something about both normal and autistic children's understanding of mind, the studies used are rather artificial and lack ecological validity.

Tasks

1 Complete Table 1 which asks you to describe each of the main cognitive theories (Piaget, Bruner and Vygotsky) and then list their strengths and weaknesses.

2 Compare and contrast theories of cognitive development. In order to do this you need to divide an A4 piece of paper in half lengthwise, and on one side list the similarities between the theories. On the other you need to state the differences. The role of social interaction and emphasis on language should be particular focal points.

3 Carry out your own research on theory of mind, especially in relation to autism. You should prepare two sides of A4 on the research involved in this area and the conclusions that can be drawn from such work.

Essay questions

"Evaluate two theories of cognitive development which attempt to show how children understand their physical and social world"

This gives you a choice option of theories to cover, although it would be extremely unwise to omit any discussion of Piaget. In order to complete a comprehensive answer you must ensure that you are familiar with the terms involved in your chosen theories and that you understand the stages of development that the child goes through. It will be insufficient simply to focus on this, however, so any description must be clear and, more importantly, concise. This will then allow you time to support your evidence using research studies, but critically you need to use such studies to show the existence of the stages of cognitive development proposed – simply copying them out of your texts will not allow you to gain the higher range of marks. To complete your essay it will then be necessary to evaluate the theories in terms of their weaknesses. Again, a list of points is not acceptable but a discussion of each weaknesses should be covered, showing that you can think in a scientific way about a child's development in this area.

"How has psychological research helped the understanding of a child's theory of mind?"

This topic has been covered only briefly in this section and both the tasks above and extra reading below are designed to expand your knowledge sufficiently to answer this question fully. This is an important topic, not only because it tells us something about a 'normal' child's cognitive development but also something about autism. In the introductory paragraph you need to make it clear that you understand the concept of theory of mind and the importance of testing using false belief tasks. Since the question specifically asks you how research has helped understanding, you should focus on certain studies, the one by Baron-Cohen, Leslie, & Frith (1985) being of most importance. You will therefore need to outline this study and, more importantly, refer back to the set question by then highlighting what it has actually told us about theory of mind. It then needs to be evaluated and any weak points considered, before a true conclusion can be drawn about the usefulness of research in this area.

Common Pitfalls

- *Students often fail to learn the terms involved in the theories of cognitive development and, more importantly, which one belongs in which period. If you don't understand the concepts behind the experiments then try them yourself!*
- *You may have worked hard to learn the tasks used by the psychologists but do not really understand why they support or criticise the theory – you must ensure that you can work this out before trying to write them up in an essay as failure to explain why they support/criticise this will costs you marks.*
- *Do not confuse the terms associated with each psychologist – the above tasks should help you clarify this.*
- *Do not emphasise Piaget at the cost of including other theorists or research – he is important but not the only view on cognitive development.*

Textbook Guide

ANTONIETTI, A., LIVERTA-SEMPIO, O., & MARCHETTI, A. (EDS) (2006). *Theory of mind and language in developmental contexts.* Springer Series on Human Exceptionality. New York: Springer-Verlag. A very recent text which looks at the links between theory of mind and language, the different levels of analysis – both intercultural and intracultural – and the interactions between them. It includes topics such as mental language and emotion, false belief tasks, social theory of mind, relationship between theory of mind and reading, silent understanding of the mind and intrapersonal theory of mind.

BARON-COHEN, S., LESLIE, A. M., & FRITH, U. (1985). Does the autistic child have a theory of mind? *Cognition 21,* 37–46. This article will provide much background concerning the research into theory of mind and is the original scientific paper in full.

GOSWAMI, U. (2004). *Handbook of childhood cognitive psychology* (Blackwell's Handbook of Developmental Psychology). Blackwell publishing. This is an up-to-date book which includes work on the origins of cognitive development, development in early childhood including theory of mind, coverage of the traditional theories of Piaget, Vygotsky and the Information Processing Approach, and also more advanced topics such as atypical development and autism.

Table 1 Theories of Cognitive Development

	Description	Strengths	Weaknesses
Piaget			
Vygotsky			
Bruner			

2.4

language development

Core areas

- Babbling
- Bruner's theory of language development
- Chomsky's nativist theory of language development
- Holophrastic stage
- Prelinguistic stage
- Preschool stage
- Skinner's learning theory of language development
- Stages of babbling
- Stages of development
- Styles of language development
- Telegraphic stage

Learning outcomes

By the end of this section you should be able to:

- outline the four stages of language development including the stages of babbling;
- describe and evaluate the explanations offered for the development of language, including nature and nurture theories and those of the interactionists (Chomsky, Skinner and Bruner respectively);
- be able to outline the styles of language development;
- thus understand the work of the key thinkers in these areas.

Running themes

- Behaviourism
- Cognitive developmental viewpoint
- Dynamic systems approach
- Information processing approach
- Nature

- Nurture
- Stage theory of development
- Transformational change
- Variational change

Introduction

Language development involves both the understanding and expression of language. D.A. Shaffer (1993) proposes that children need four kinds of knowledge about language in order to achieve this: knowledge of phonology, semantics, syntax and pragmatics, or, more simply, information regarding the sound, meaning, grammar and rules of language.

> *As we shall go on to see, children do generally acquire skills in this particular order.*

Stages of language development

Prelinguistic

Even within the womb it is predicted that the child can hear and recognise sound, especially its mother's voice. De Casper and Spence (1986) asked mothers to read a passage of text from a children's book in late pregnancy and found that after birth such babies would alter their sucking rate in order to hear this, compared to a control group.

> *After birth preference is shown for familiar speech sounds/the human voice rather than other sounds.*

Biological evidence to indicate an innate ability to process speech comes from studies which show that it is processed by the right hemisphere of the brain, and from the ability to distinguish between speech sounds/phonemes. Eimas et al. (1971) demonstrated this and some evidence has also suggested that even newborns can potentially discriminate between phonemes (see Eimas – 1974), although this does not become language specific until at least 8 months.

The development of babbling (use of vocalisation without particular meaning, although showing speech-like sounds) after 4 months is a fundamental stage in language development (see the work of key thinkers below). Babbling will reflect the language heard around the infant.

Holophrastic (McNeill, 1970)

This is the 'one-word stage' but before children produce words they will show many signs of understanding them (usually at 7–8 months names of familiar others and self will be understood, for instance). Overall research (Fenson et al., 1990) indicates that girls understand more than boys and there is a developmental (vocabulary) spurt at about 12 months. Children produce their first word around 10 months. This work was derived from using the MacArthur Communicative Development Inventories (CDI), which are checklists examining development from 8–28 months old, using infant and toddler scales, focusing on early gestures and then word production.

Initially psychologists believed that early words were only produced within a specific context (were context-bound), but later work has suggested that children can use them in more than one context.

Telegraphic (approximately 18 months)

Two-word phrases are produced involving nouns and verbs but excluding function words ('a'), plurals and tenses.

According to Braine (1963), pivot and open words are included, that is, words that tend to appear in either the same, or different, places in speech.

Brown (1973) suggested that telegraphic speech is based on a basic rule order involving an agent + action + object + location.

Preschool period

By 2 years children combine words into utterances which can be measured using the MLU, or mean length of utterances. Using the CDI, Fenson et al. (1994) found that the average length of a sentence ranged from nearly two morphemes at 16 months to around eight at 30 months.

By the end of their second year children understand something of the pattern of language and the form of words (that is, an understanding of morphology). At 16 months children understand little of grammatical rules, acquire a knowledge of half of them by age 2, and by 2.5 years most children can apply all of them – that is, the use of regular noun plurals and the possessive, as well as the progressive ('-ing') and past tense. Such rules can help the modification of nouns and verbs respectively with those relevant to nouns applied first.

By 2.5 years much change in the use of language is evident. Speech becomes longer, more complex and contains more grammatical morphemes, including prepositions, prefixes and suffixes. Over-generalisation tends to occur where rules are used in situations in which they do not apply, although as the years progress children become more adept at saying things which fit the situation (show pragmatics).

Anglin (1993) estimated that a 6-year-old child has a vocabulary of nearly 11,000 words, which rises to 20,000 at age 8 and then doubles by the age of 10 years although, naturally, there will always be individual variation.

REMEMBER

Language is believed to develop in four phases:

➤ *Prelinguistic* – the most important aspect of which is babbling.
➤ *Holophrastic* – which is the stage of one-word development.
➤ *Telegraphic* – where two-word phrases are produced involving nouns and verbs but excluding function words ('a'), plurals and tenses.
➤ *Preschool development* – where speech becomes longer, more complex and contains more grammatical morphemes including prepositions, prefixes and suffixes.

Key thinkers

Skinner (1957) – learning theory

Skinner used his principles of operant conditioning and applied them to the development of language. In other words, he saw language merely as a product of trial and error, reinforcement and behaviour-shaping. Reinforcement comes from the environment, for example a parent smiling in response to sound production. Imitation may also be involved, where the child tries to repeat something it has just heard (echoic response), the child may be rewarded for similar production of a word (a tact) or learns a word that has personal significance (a mand). More specifically, phonemes are acquired while babbling and as echoic responses, whereby parents reinforce sounds that are recognisable while ignoring others, thus making these phonemes more likely to be repeated. During the babbling phase phonemes are combined to make morphemes as a process of trial and error and are again reinforced by others until such behaviour-shaping produces words. This process continues until words are shaped into telegraphic two-word utterances, phrases and sentences.

Chomsky (1959) – nativist theory

Chomsky had a very different view from Skinner, as he believed that language acquisition was innate and that children automatically learn it because they have an inbuilt mechanism that allows them to interpret/de-code the language they hear and its rules. Known as the language acquisition device (LAD), recognition of 'linguistic universals' becomes possible. A distinction was made between the surface and deep structure of sentences, that is the actual phrases used versus their meaning. Chomsky suggested that the LAD further allows for the transformation of grammar such that the deep structure can be obtained from the surface structure. In 1986 Chomsky updated his theory and proposed the idea of a universal grammar rather than the LAD – the idea being that linguistic universals found in most languages allow for the innate interpretation of language.

Bruner (1975)

The form of language is related to the social world and the routines that take place within it, as society helps provide a context for the meaning of words. However it does not aid morphology (the form or structure of words) or syntax (grammar).

Oller (1980) and Stark (1980) – stages in the development of babbling

They proposed that a sequence of stages emerges:

1. 0–2 months – reflexive vocalisation – sounds are made in order to indicate distress, discomfort or bodily processes.

2. 2–4 months – sounds are used for the purposes of communication, for example, laughing.

3 4–7 months – vocal stage – loudness and pitch vary and vocalisations are more frequent. Greater control over vocal apparatus becomes possible due to the child's physical maturation.

4 6 months – canonical babbling - recognisable syllables emerge.

5 8 months – duplicated babbling – babbling results in the production of repeated sounds (da-da).

6 11 months – variegated babbling/ non-reduplicated babbling – here different sound combinations are produced (da-de)

Nelson (1973) – styles of language development

Nelson proposed that the development of either an expressive or referential style of language development is related to the words then produced, with children using action words and people's names if adopting an expressive style, or object names if using a referential style.

REMEMBER

Theories of language development:

➢ Skinner saw language merely as a product of trial and error, reinforcement and behaviour-shaping.
➢ Chomsky believed that language acquisition was innate and that children automatically learn it because they have an inbuilt mechanism that allows them to interpret/de-code the language they hear and its rules.
➢ According to Bruner the form of language is related to the social world and the routines that take place within it, as society helps provide a context for the meaning of words.

Handy Hints for evaluating the work of key thinkers

• Skinner's theory cannot account for the universal stages that children seem to go through in language development, nor does it account for the similar errors made by children, for example, 'mouses' rather than 'mice' – language must therefore involve more than simply reinforcement.

- It would also be difficult to accept that the vast language produced by children, and the creativity of such language is a result of only trial and error.
- Chomsky's theory has many strengths but it does ignore the active role parents play in language development, or any possible role they have in learning.
- Interactionists criticise the idea that language is purely innate and propose that at least some social interaction/stimulation is required to acquire the meaning of words within the correct context.
- Bruner (1983) alternatively proposed that children have a LASS (language acquisition support system) where language derives from the interaction between parent and child, most notably by giving language the necessary social context.

Tasks

1 There are a number of definitions which are critical to understanding this topic/section. While you will not need to provide definitions within an essay itself, it will help you gain confidence. Therefore write down the definitions of all of the following words: phonology, semantics, syntax, pragmatics, babbling, function words, plurals, tenses, pivot words, open words, MLU, prepositions, prefixes, suffixes, morphology, grammatical morphemes, operant conditioning, a tact, a mand, LAD.

2 Draw a time-line to represent the stages of a child's language development.

3 There are some interesting studies on the prelinguistic stage of development which have been beyond the scope of this section. It will help your overall understanding of the topic if you can research some of these. Consider focusing on how the studies were carried out and how sucking techniques and heart rate can indicate linguistic understanding.

Essay questions

"What does psychological research tell us about the stages involved in the development of language?"

Notice that this question is not simply asking you to list the stages of language development, although an outline of the stages is implicit in the question and the time-line you have completed in the tasks above should aid you to do this. Initially you need a clear idea of the sequence in which things happen but you need to demonstrate how such stages develop, using supporting evidence rather than general summaries. For each area of development the question therefore asks you to provide detail about studies carried out into each stage, how they were done and what they have shown. Since a good developmental psychologist is required to focus on such work in a critical way, it is also necessary to then raise any issues surrounding such work and to highlight the issue that, despite the evidence provided, there will always be individual differences in the ages at which the stages are experienced by children and the types of development they show.

❝Describe and evaluate theories of language development❞

There are several general theories that could be covered in this question and this book has only provided you with three of the key theories, although there are others. In a timed essay, however, you will need to be focused and although you could expand this outline using extra research, it will provide you with the guiding principles needed to write on this topic. In any introduction you should draw a distinction between the various perspectives that can be taken, that is, the theorists who believe that language is an innate process, those who believe it is a result of learning and those who sit somewhere in between, with the social context at least providing guidance on the rules of language. It will be necessary to outline the key aspects of each theory and to provide some detail on the research from which such conclusions could be drawn. Since this will, however, only provide you with descriptive marks you will then need to focus on the strengths and weaknesses of each theory in order to gain analytical marks. You may want to focus on the general nature versus nurture argument, directly on the principles each theorist applied to their explanation or more specifically on aspects of their research. This should enable you to make both an informative and balanced answer to this question.

Common Pitfalls

- *One of the commonest pitfalls students fall into is a failure to understand the language used in this topic, and Task 1 is specifically designed to ensure you have a good basis from which to proceed with the developments presented.*
- *Make sure that you have more than a simple list of dates at which developments occur, and expand your knowledge by supporting it with research into the stages of development.*

- *Remember these stages of development are not prescriptive and there will always be individual differences within them.*
- *Theories of language development need to be looked at critically and you should ensure you are able to outline their strengths and weaknesses, not just what they propose.*

Textbook Guide

BARRETT, M. (1999). *The development of language.* Hove, UK: Psychology Press. Various aspects of language development are covered in a very clear and understandable fashion.

CHOMSKY, N. (1986). *Knowledge of language: its nature, origin and use.* New York: Praeger. A very useful text if you have a particular interest in Chomsky's view on language.

HARLEY, T. A. (2001). *The psychology of language: from data to theory* (2nd ed.). Hove, UK: Psychology Press. A comprehensive text which focuses on various aspects touched on in this section.

2.5	
physical/motor development	

Core areas

- Apgar score
- Brain
- Cephalocaudal development
- Genotype
- Glia
- Growth hormone
- Maturation
- Motor development
- Muscular development
- Myelinisation

- Nervous system
- Physical development
- Pincer grip
- Proximodistal development
- Puberty
- Skeletal development
- Ulnar grasp

Learning outcomes

By the end of this section you should be able to:

- define and understand the terms above;
- outline the key areas of physical development that undergo change during the lifespan including height and weight, skeletal and muscular development, changes to the brain and nervous system and those that occur at the time of puberty;
- identify the changes that occur in motor ability throughout the lifespan including pre-natally;
- identify research to support these changes;
- acknowledge the role of emotional factors in these areas of development and the individual nature of such changes.

Running themes

- Cognitive-developmental viewpoint
- Connectionist approach
- Ethology
- Nature
- Nurture
- Stage theory of development
- Transformational change
- Variational change

Introduction

The rate of maturation is an inheritable characteristic and development will also be influenced by our genotype – that is our inherited and unique combination of genes. Growth will be further influenced by hormones, most critically by the work of the pituitary gland which regulates the endocrine system and produces a growth hormone (GH) that stimulates growth and development.

When babies are born, an Apgar score is taken to establish basic physical condition. A score is given for heart rate, respiration, colour, muscle tone and reflexes to determine whether or not further attention needs to be given to these areas in the post-natal period.

Key theories/stages of physical development

There are subsequently several areas of physical development that should be considered:

Physical development: height and weight

Growth rate in the first two years is considerable, with birth weight often doubling by 6 months and tripling by the end of the first year. However, since this rate of growth would be unsustainable, from this point to puberty it slows, averaging 2–3 inches in height and 6–7 pounds in weight each year (D.R. Shaffer, 1993).

Physical development: skeletal and muscular development

Skeletal development varies, with skull and hands maturing first and most structures in place by the age of 18. According to Tanner (1978) neonates are born with all the muscle cells they will ever have, with muscular development occurring in a cephalocaudal direction, that is, from top to toes.

Physical development: the brain and nervous system

The newborn's head is 70 per cent of adult size at birth, and then maturation and growth proceed in a cephalocaudal way, although this will be complemented by proximodistal development, where growth also extends from the centre of the body outwards. The brain is, however, only 25 per cent of its prospective adult weight, although by age 5 approximately 90 per cent weight has been achieved.

Neurons are vital for the development of the brain and nervous system. They develop through the process of mitosis, and are usually fully formed by birth, although as many as half of those produced early in life subsequently die (Janowsky & Finlay, 1986). The neurons also take on many functions in the early years due to their plasticity or capacity for change which will be shaped by environmental factors/experience. This was demonstrated by the findings of Riesen's (1950) study of chimps who were raised in the dark and it was found that the deprivation they had therefore experienced prevented neural and visual development, highlighting the role of experience in physical development. The nerve cells that nourish these neurons, insulate them and facilitate the transmission of neural impulses (glia), also develop during the prenatal period (myelinisation occurs) but then continue the process until at least 2 years of age (Tanner, 1978).

The brain stem and midbrain are mostly developed at birth and allow the child to display reflexive behaviours as basic biological functions. Subsequent development occurs in the cerebrum, most notably in the primary motor and primary sensory areas of the brain, such that motor development matures, as do senses such as sight, sound, smell and taste.

Recent theories would postulate that the left and right hemispheres of the brain assume different functions, such that the left engages in processes concerned with speech, hearing, verbal memory, decision-making and language while the right is more focused on visuo-spatial processing, sensation and emotion. Children will tend, however, to show lateral preferences.

Physical development: puberty

Physical development shows a significant change at puberty – defined as the point where sexual maturity is reached. In girls this is easier to define as it is marked by the first menstrual period (menarche) and increased breast size, while in boys it is more subtle and marked by growing penis and testicles, change in voice and, in both cases, growth of pubic hair. A growth spurt will also occur in both sexes, although this will generally be later in boys than girls and takes the form of increases in both height and weight.

> *Physical development is obviously a biological process of maturation, but it will also be influenced by factors such as nutrition, illness, emotional factors and stress, leading to failure to thrive.*

Physical development:

➤ The key areas of physical development that undergo change involve those in height and weight, skeletal and muscular development, those to the brain and nervous system and the changes that occur at the time of puberty.

Key theories/stages of motor development

Harris and Butterworth (2004) provide excellent summary tables of the stages of motor development in children, ranging through the pre-natal period to the post-natal.

A general adapted summary of what happens in the pre-natal period is provided below:

WEEK	MOTOR PATTERN
3	No movement but nerve cells present and some aspects of nervous system.
7	Limited research indicates small foetal movement.
8	General writhing movements and a startle response of indistinctive sequence occur. Spinal cord present but not yet separated.
9	Hiccups can occur, as can isolated arm or leg movements and limited head, jaw and tongue movements.
10	Hand-to-face contact is possible, as is rotation of the body. Connections established between sensory fibres and interneurons.
11	Stretches and yawns may be observed. Significant increase of motor neurone synapses.
12	Fingers move. *(Cont'd)*

14	Hand rotates. Connection of neurons to major parts of body become more developed and myelinisation occurs.
16	There is extension of the body.
18	Eye movements occur.
24	Thumb-sucking may take place.

By the age of 1 month the child starts to show development of muscles by lifting its chin up while lying flat and will then progress though a series of stages that will allow it to lift it's chest and even sit up if supported. Since (as we have seen above) development is cephalocaudal, motor development also occurs from the head downwards and therefore there will be more motor movements in the top half of the body before the lower – for example, lifting the head before walking.

The reflex to grasp objects appears even in the initial stages of life but young infants use their sight to initiate and then guide hand movements to grasp objects. From 6 months onwards the ulnar grasp (holding using fingers against the palm) extends to the pincer grip, where the thumb is used in opposition to the fingers, facilitating more manipulation of objects. As maturation occurs the child becomes able to walk, run and then hop, skip and so on, until they become more purposeful in their movements and display greater control over limbs. Eye-to-hand co-ordination also improves rapidly during the pre-school years.

The following list indicates the motor development of infants in sequential order.

- 2 months – able to lift head up on his own
- 3 months – can roll over
- 4 months – can sit propped up without falling over
- 6 months – is able to sit up without support
- 7 months – begins to stand while holding on to things for support
- 9 months – can begin to walk, still using support
- 10 months – is able to stand momentarily on her own without support
- 11 months – can stand alone with more confidence
- 12 months – begins walking alone without support
- 14 months – can walk backwards without support
- 17 months – can walk up steps with little or no support
- 18 months – able to manipulate objects with feet while walking, such as kicking a ball

(reference: http://allpsych.com/psychology101/developmental.htm).

Handy Hints for evaluating information on physical and motor development

- Remember that all of the information provided is simply guidelines based on the standard for development but this does not mean that all individuals will progress at the same rate.
- The impact of psychological and social factors may be as important for physical and motor development as biological ones.
- As research identifies new techniques for examining physical development and the role of the brain, we will be able to increase our understanding of these areas.

Tasks

1 Draw time-lines to represent the stages of both physical and motor development in children as this will help you consolidate your own knowledge and understanding and will also be a useful revision tool.

2 You are attending a parent education group that wishes to know what they can expect from their children as they develop physically throughout their lives. Prepare a presentation outlining the key issues, providing them with examples of how they could extend each area of development with their child, where possible. Practise this presentation on members of your tutor group.

3 Using your textbooks, research studies to support the stages of physical and motor development you have learned about. You should outline each one and then highlight exactly what type and stage of development the study supports.

Essay questions

"The physical and motor development of the child is an ongoing process. Discuss"

This essay allows you to write an opening introduction which generally defines the process of maturation and the nature–nurture debate within this context. You then need to outline the stages of development that occur and the kinds of physical and motor changes a child might experience throughout its lifespan, including the key areas such as developments in height and weight, skeletal and muscular development, the changes that occur to the brain and nervous system and those that precede puberty. The increase in motor control from the stage of lifting one's head to grasping small objects or running should also be examined, and wherever possible grounded within a research context since it will otherwise simply read like a list of chronological facts. Before concluding that these developments always occur in individuals, you should take a critical approach to the evidence and address the impact that environmental factors such as nutrition, illness and emotional experience might have, as well acknowledging the individual variations that may occur in these patterns. Only by addressing all of these issues can an overall conclusion be drawn.

Common Pitfalls

- *The first obvious mistake to avoid is the mixing up of areas of development and you must be sure that you understand the differences (and the similarities) between physical and motor development.*
- *Also do not assume that the stages covered are set in stone – remember they are simply guidelines and not every individual will experience them at either the ages given or even in the same set sequence, and this should be explicitly acknowledged.*
- *Another common mistake is to assume that all developments in these areas occur because of some biological basis, ignoring the role of the environment and experience. Gerhardt's text below seeks to draw these different views together and will help you avoid making this assumption.*

Textbook Guide

GALLAHUE, D. L., AND OZMON, J. C. (2005). *Understanding motor development: infants, children, adolescents, adults.* McGraw-Hill Education. This text examines motor development across the lifespan and looks at up-to-date research and theory using a conceptual framework, including biological, affective, cognitive and behavioural aspects.

GERHARDT, S. (2004). *Why love matters: how affection shapes a baby's brain.* Blunner Routledge. This book encompasses the nature-nurture theme that has been raised throughout this Course Companion and explains scientifically how sensitivity to a baby's needs and a caring response can actually affect how a baby's nervous system develops. It thus draws together links between neuroscience, psychology and biochemistry in the field of physical and motor development.

www.who.int/childgrowth/standards/motor-milestones/en/index.htm
This website provided by the World Health Organisation provides tables and graphs presenting the standards of achievement of the six gross motor milestones.

2.6	
biological/hereditary influences on development	

Core areas

- Behavioural genetics
- Co-dominance
- Chromosomal and genetic abnormalities
- Chromosomes
- Extroversion
- Family studies
- Genotype
- Introversion
- IQ
- Meiosis
- Mitosis
- Modifier genes
- Phenotype
- Selective breeding
- Zygotes

Learning outcomes

By the end of this section you should be able to:

- define key terms;
- understand the processes and methods involved in investigating the biological basis for behaviour;
- outline how genes influence behaviour;
- acknowledge the work of the key thinkers in this area;
- outline the process of hereditary transmission;
- consider the range of chromosomal and genetic abnormalities/disorders that occur;
- describe and evaluate hereditary influences on IQ and personality.

Running themes

- Ecological validity
- Ethology
- Ethics
- Nature
- Nurture

Introduction

Sir Francis Galton (1822–1911) was the first scientist to study heredity and human behaviour systematically. Human behavioural genetics attempts to understand both the genetic and environmental contributions to individual variations in human behaviour. (http://www.ornl.gov/sci/techresources/human_genome/elsi/behaviour.shtml)

> This is tricky because it is often difficult to define the behaviour in question especially as behaviours involve multiple genes.

There are a number of indications that behaviour has a biological basis (McInerney, 1999):

- Behaviour often is species specific.
- Behaviours often breed true. We can reproduce behaviours in successive generations of organisms. Behaviours change in response to alterations in biological structures or processes.
- In humans, some behaviours run in families.
- Behaviour has an evolutionary history that persists across related species.

Methods of study in behavioural genetics

Traditional research strategies in behavioural genetics include:

- **Selective breeding** – researchers try to selectively breed certain attributes in animals.
- **Family studies** – studies of twins and adoptees, techniques designed to sort biological from environmental influences. The idea behind this is that if a characteristic is due to hereditary factors then similarity should increase with kinship. It

also, therefore, helps estimate the influence of environmental factors. Since twins share similar (or identical genes) they are a useful source of information in this area. A heritability coefficient can be used to estimate the amount of variation that is attributable to hereditary factors where the heritability of an attribute equals the correlation between identical twins minus the correlation between fraternal (non-identical) twins, multiplied by two (Plomin et al., 1980). So, H = (r identical twins − r fraternal twins) × 2.

- **Biometric model** – data from different familial relationships can be combined in a comprehensive model that includes both genetic and environmental influences and, in more complex versions, genotype–environment correlation and interaction. In addition, a greater variety of models of genetic and environmental transmission can be formally contrasted, and more accurate parameter estimates can be obtained, than is the case with the more conventional methods based on piecemeal examination of familial correlations
- **QTL analysis** – the development of genetic linkage maps means that attention is now focused on the identification of susceptibility genes for common, complex disorders.
- **DNA** – can be analysed to determine its association with particular behaviours, for example the genes associated with major mental illnesses such as schizophrenia and bipolar disorder.
- **Genetics and molecular biology** – have provided some significant insights into behaviours associated with inherited disorders. We also know the steps from gene to effect for a number of single-gene disorders that result in mental retardation, including phenylketonuria (PKU).

Handy Hints for evaluating the role of heritability (see D. R. Shaffer, 1993)

- Hereditability largely ignores the role of non-hereditary, environmental factors and their influence on development.
- Heritable does not mean inherited, that is, the estimates apply to populations not the development of specific individuals.
- It refers to the extent to which differences among individuals on any attribute are related to differences in the genes they have inherited.

How do genes influence behaviour?

No single gene determines a particular behaviour. Behaviours are complex traits involving multiple genes and are affected by a variety of other factors, such as, for example environmental ones. The presence of certain genetic factors can enhance or repress other genetic factors. In addition, the protein encoded by a gene can be modified in ways that can affect its ability to carry out its normal cellular function.

Having a genetic variant doesn't necessarily mean that a particular trait will develop. Parents contribute to their child's development not only by passing on their genes but also by structuring an environment which may foster them. Scarr and McCartney (1983) suggest that the environments parents provide will depend on their own genotype. Genetic factors also can influence the role of certain environmental factors in the development of a particular trait. Their ideas on the evocative genotype/environment interactions propose that a child's heritable characteristics will affect others' behaviour towards the child and they will seek others within their environment who are compatible with such traits (active gene influences).

Three models of genetic transmission of phenotypes (the observable physical or biochemical characteristics of an organism) from parents to children include (Reiss, 1997):

- **The Passive Model:** genetic effects are attributed to the 50 per cent overlap in genes between a parent and biological child.
- **Evocative Models:**
  (a) **Child-Effects Model:** genes cause given behaviour in the child, which then causes the parent's reaction. In this model, what the parent does does not matter in the development of behaviour.
  (b) **Parent-Effects Model:** genes cause the child's temperament, which causes the parent's response, which causes given behaviour in the child. In this model, what the parent does *does* matter in the development of behaviour.

D.R. Shaffer (1993) therefore summarises the complex interactions we see in this section as ones where genotypes and environments combine to produce developmental change and where differences combine to produce varying developmental outcomes. While genes exert some influence over the environments we experience, the availability of environments will also limit the possible phenotypes likely to emerge from a particular genotype.

Key thinkers

Swammerdam

First proposed a preformation theory which stated that each sperm cell contained a tiny 'preformed' embryo or homunculus that was nourished by the female egg and would grow in the womb.

Wolff (1759/1959)

Recognised that the sperm and egg join and then divide many times but still contain some of the genetic make-up of both parents.

Mendel (1865)

Made several key contributions. Namely that:

- Genes are transmitted through generations.
- Inherited characteristics are determined by a pair of genes, one of which is inherited from each parent. When a parent produces a gamete the gene pair for each attribute divides so that each gamete has one member of the pair (law of segregation).
- There will often be a dominant gene. For example, the gene for brown eye colour is dominant and blue recessive. A person who contains two genes of the same kind is homozygous for the attribute, while inheriting two different ones makes them heterozygous.

Morgan (1933)

Discovered chromosomes, of which there are 46 pairs in the nucleus of cells and whose structure is made up of genes.

Waddington (1966)

Introduced the idea of canalisation where genes operate in such a way that they limit or restrict development to a small number of outcomes.

Gottesman (1963)

Initiated a range-of-reaction principle suggesting that one's genotype sets limits on the range of phenotypes one could possibly exhibit in response to different environments. So the genotype essentially determines the types of outcomes that would be usual for a given attribute but the environment determines the point within the range where the individual will actually fall.

Hereditary transmission

- Ovulation occurs and the uniting of a sperm and egg leads to conception.
- The sperm soon disintegrates, which results in its 23 chromosomes being released to unite with the 23 from the ovum. This leads to the formation of a zygote containing thousands of genes that will lead to that human being's make-up.

- Reproduction occurs through mitosis where the cell duplicates its chromosomes and then divides into two genetically identical cells. All body cells are the result of this process.
- Meiosis is the process in which a germ cell divides to produce gametes containing half of each parent's set of chromosomes so these combinations and the crossing-over principle leads to individuality, that is, the point at which genetic material in chromosomes is exchanged. For example, gender is determined by the 23rd chromosome. If an X chromosome meets another X then a child will be female, while XY constitutes a male.
- However the genes one inherits (one's genotype) may be expressed in various ways (which affects one's phenotype, or the way that person feels, behaves etc.).
- Co-dominance occurs when the phenotype of the heterozygous individual contains an exact combination of the two inherited genes.

> *Modifier genes can influence the expression of other genes and most complex behaviours are actually the result of the interaction of many genes, not just of one pair (thus we have polygenic traits).*

Chromosomal and genetic abnormalities

Congenital defects may be present at birth and be the result of chromosomal or genetic abnormalities. Various procedures can be used to determine defects in advance, including amniocentesis, chronic villus sampling and ultrasound techniques. Genetic counselling may also be offered.

REMEMBER

Causes of abnormalities

➤ Although there may be other explanations, generally *autosomal abnormalities* occur when an abnormal sperm or ovum carrying an extra autosome combines with a normal gamete to form a zygote that has 47 chromosomes, so a trisomy occurs (it contains three chromosomes of that type).

➤ *Chromosomal abnormalities* are usually the result of an uneven segregation of chromosomes during mitosis and meiosis.

➤ *Genetic defects* can be caused by recessive genes or mutations where a change in the chemical structure or arrangement of one or more genes produces a new phenotype.

Any full discussion of these is beyond the scope of this section so a table is provided below giving an outline of hereditary disorders.

Table 2 Hereditary Disorders

Disorder	Cause of abnormality
Turner's syndrome	Occurs when an ovum containing no X chromosome is fertilised by an X-bearing sperm. Phenotypically female but infertile.
Klinefelter syndrome	Occurs with an imbalance in X chromosomes where two X from the ovum combine with a Y-bearing sperm. Phenotypically male but with some female characteristics.
Fragile-X syndrome	The X chromosome is compressed or broken leading to this sex chromosome abnormality. Can cause mental retardation in males.
Down' syndrome	An extra 21st chromosome causes this abnormality. Some retardation.
Cystic fibrosis	Child lacks an enzyme that prevents mucous from obstructing the lungs and digestive tract.
Muscular dystrophy	A disease which attacks the muscles, resulting in loss of motor abilities and affects speech.
Phenylketonuria	The enzyme necessary to digest foods is lacking. Can cause retardation and hyperactivity if not treated.
Haemophilia	Child lacks a substance that causes the blood to clot. Mainly occurs in males.
Diabetes	The individual is unable to metabolise sugar properly as too little insulin is produced by the body. Can be sex-linked.

Hereditary influences on IQ and personality

In general, it is easier to discern the relationship between biology and behaviour for chromosomal and single-gene disorders than for common, complex behaviours such as personality traits,

Researchers in the field of behavioural genetics have asserted claims for a genetic basis of numerous physical behaviours, including homosexuality, aggression, impulsivity and nurturing. A growing scientific and popular focus on genes and behaviour has contributed to a resurgence of behavioural genetic determinism – the belief that genetics is the major factor in determining behaviour (McInerney, 1999; Rothstein, 1999). In a text such as this only brief reference can be made to this vast area and the brief discussion is focused on the hereditary influences on IQ and personality, although there are an infinite number of areas that could be examined, as mentioned in the introduction to this section. This is because research indicates that these factors show some resemblance/commonality that increases as kinship increases.

Hereditary influences on IQ

Generally studies of twins reveal that identical twins, even when reared apart, are more similar in IQ than fraternal twins reared together and this has been consistently found even in longitudinal studies. However the environment inevitably influences IQ by providing stimulation and learning opportunities, such that intellectual similarities are found among members of the same household even in the absence of genetic relatedness. Scarr and Weinberg (1976, 1983), for example, found that while adopted children were more closely related to their biological parents than to their adopted ones, interracial siblings showed some intellectual similarities. Thus, one's phenotype for intelligence can be influenced by environmental factors.

Hereditary influences on personality

Selective breeding studies indicate that temperamental characteristics such as fearfulness and sociability have a strong genetic basis (Plomin et al., 1980) and many similar personality traits are more observable in identical than non-identical twins. Two of the most heritable traits in adult personality types seem to be introversion and extroversion (shy and anxious types versus highly sociable individuals). Importantly, Rowe and Plomin (1981) argue that the environmental influences that contribute to personality are those that make individuals different from each other, that is, non-shared environmental influences (for example the different treatment of siblings within the same household). They propose that the effects of the non-shared environment on personality characteristics can be described using the equation

$$NSE = 1 - r \text{ (correlation for identical twins on that attribute)}$$

So because identical twins have the same genes, the only explanation for any differences must be environmental. The current view in personality research predicts that while some traits in personality are the result of genetic factors there are others that result from learning.

Tasks

1 Draw a flow diagram to represent the processes involved in hereditary transmission.

2 Use your textbook to look up current research into hereditary influences on personality, IQ and mental illness. For each area produce an A4 sheet summarising the main aims, procedures, findings, conclusions and criticisms of the work.

3 Write down a description of yourself – this could include both physical and psychological characteristics. As a behavioural geneticist use your knowledge of this area to discuss this make-up.

Essay questions

"Discuss the effects of hereditary influences on development"

As this essay title looks at development as a whole, you have the option of covering the fundamental biological processes involved but also the types of disorders that result from abnormalities. Such data would lean towards a purely hereditary basis for development so you then need to balance the argument by showing that it may actually be an interplay between nature and nurture. There are many examples for you to discuss, some covered in this section, but many more that are not can be developed by your further reading. There are all sorts of issues you may want to cover, as diverse as hereditary influences on criminality, homosexuality and mental illness. Whichever issues you choose, the underlying premise must be that there is at least some hereditary influence on behaviour, although the extent to which that dominates development should be viewed with caution since environmental factors cannot be ignored. Showing that you understand this, and highlighting the point with research examples will increase your evaluation skills and show the examiner that you look beyond the bare facts.

Common Pitfalls

- *Failure to understand the basic terms and process involved in the biology of behaviour will significantly impair your overall understanding of this area and you therefore need to ensure you have these basics in place before proceeding with further reading or writing in the area.*
- *Do not assume that there is only a genetic basis to behaviour and that all characteristics can be explained by inheritance. The contribution they make towards determining one's environment, or indeed the role of the environment itself, must be considered.*
- *Failing to research the extensive findings on the contribution of heredity to wider areas than has been possible here will lead to a very narrow insight in the area.*
- *As new techniques for investigating genetics emerge, developments in this field rapidly progress and you need to be aware of this.*

Textbook Guide

EYSENCK, H. J. (1990). Genetic and environmental contributions to individual differences: the three major dimensions of personality. *Journal of Personality, 58,* 245–261. The hereditary influences on personality are discussed by one of the experts in the field.

PLOMIN R., MCLEARN G. E., DEFRIES, J. C. & RUTTER, M. (2000). *Behavioural genetics: a primer.* New York: W. H. Freeman. An introductory text with a focus on what we know about genetics in psychology. It is divided into sections on cognitive disabilities, psychopathology, personality, health psychology and biopsychology, and the environment, and emphasizes the clinical aspects of behavioural genetics that are interesting to students, as well as new technological advances.

RUTTER, M. (2005). *Genes and behaviour: nature–nurture interplay explained.* Blackwell publishing. Rutter provides a balanced and authoritative overview of the genetic revolution and its implications for understanding human behaviour. He sets out in lay person's terms what genetic science has discovered to date, explaining exactly what genes do, how much is nature and how much is nurture. He argues that nature and nurture are not truly separate, giving powerful illustrations of how the two interact to determine our behaviour. He also considers the implications of genetic findings for policy and practice.

2.7	
social influences on development	

Core areas

- Cognitive socialisation
- Emotional socialisation
- Family
- Parental styles
- Peers
- Socialisation
- Symbolic play
- Zone of proximal development

Learning outcomes

By the end of this section you should be able to:

- define the key concepts;
- understand what is involved in the process of socialisation;
- be able to recognise the general contribution that parents make to this process, including to the social, cognitive and moral development of the child;
- examine the research evidence about the role peers play in development;
- outline the various kinds of play and the theories surrounding its contribution to development;
- evaluate the social influence of parents/peers on development.

Running themes

- Behaviourism
- Cognitive-developmental viewpoint
- Dynamic systems approach
- Ecological validity
- Nurture
- Psychoanalytic viewpoint
- Transformational change
- Variational change

Introduction

The social influences on development are many and varied, but just three specific areas will be focused on in this section – the role of parents/family, peers and play. Throughout this book there have been references which implicitly show the social influences that some of these may have, and this work will not be repeated here. You will therefore need to cross-reference, for example, the initial role of the mother in the acquisition of early social behaviours (such as smiling) and the role of peers and play in the social acquisition of gender roles (see sections 2.10 and 2.9 for more detail).

> Socialisation refers to the process by which the individual child adapts to the social order into which it is born and is the means by which the child becomes a full participating member of society. The child has to acquire many different skills and capabilities in order to become socialised. It has, for example, to be able to enter into relationships, acquire social skills, show an ability to interpret the mental states of others, and understand social structures, moral standards and values. These skills are learned from the important social agents mentioned above, for example, parents, peers, school, etc.

Parents/family

It is beyond the scope of this book to cover every area of development which parents can affect. Research on the subject is wide-ranging and looks at lots of possible areas: altruism, anti-social behaviour, obesity, mental illness – just to list a few of the more diverse. Families are important for cognitive and emotional socialisation, for providing an introduction to pro- and anti-social behaviours and moral development, as well as providing learning opportunities about basic routines. The aim of this section is simply to introduce the idea, and it therefore takes a somewhat more general view. Family here is used to refer to the various types that exist and a discussion on the types and nature of family can be researched if it is an area of interest to you. The traditional nuclear family (consisting of mother, father, child) has long been replaced and now family units may be those with single or same-sex parents, step-parents or even extended families. Each plays a role in the development of the child.

LeVine (1974) states that families have three basic roles to play – the survival goal which aids the physical development and safety of the child, the economic goal ensuring that they have the necessary skills to support themselves economically as they grow, and lastly the self-actualisation goal aimed at helping them achieve their full potential. These operate in a hierarchical way since one's full potential cannot be achieved unless basic survival needs are initially met.

Inevitably attachment is the basis from which this section starts but it will not be covered in detail since section 2.10 considers the role of the mother in facilitating early sociability, looking at the role of attachment specifically. Critically, however, attachment research shows that a child who has a secure attachment will benefit from a sense of security, which provides them with a safe base from which to explore the world, as well as a positive internal working model of themselves. Warm and sensitive mothers are most likely to encourage this type of attachment.

D.R. Shaffer (1993: 573) summarises the influence of warm and responsive parents as follows:

Children who are securely attached at an early age:

- are competent and confident students at school age
- are altruistic
- are generally obedient and have good relationships with parents and peers
- have high self-esteem
- respond well to reasonable discipline
- have good role-taking skills
- are happy with their gender identity

To give just one example of research into this area, Hazan and Shaver (1987) have found that a child's attachment style in early life correlates with their later experience of adult romantic love, whereby securely attached infants go on to have happy and lasting relationships while insecure types found relationships were more difficult and believed true love was rare.

Peers

Throughout the lifespan contact with family decreases and time spent with peers increases. Even in the initial years, for example, a child's contact with peers extends from 10 per cent of the time at age 2 to 30 per cent of the time at school age. Inevitably the level of social influence of peers will also therefore increase. In the preschool years children establish friendships and gravitate towards children with similar interests, behaviours, ages and often same-sex formations, as gender differences in play are quite marked at this stage of life. Thus peers act as reinforcing agents and social role models, and as Lamb et al. (1980) found, they will actively reinforce gender-appropriate behaviours. Similarity is important as it provides a safe base from which new ideas and behaviours can be tested.

Hartup (1996) stated that friendships have four features:

- Children know each other well and have similar interests, so can communicate easily.
- They require and offer similar levels of support, which encourages a sense of equality.
- There is a positive environment to thrash out problems.
- They share common aims and goals.

Furthermore, she argues (1983) that mixed-age interactions are critical for social and personality development as they help the child acquire new skills. Overall research suggests that more pro-social behaviour occurs in mixed-age groups compared to more anti-social behaviour in same-age groups.

Interestingly, research has found that when monkeys are raised without peer support and only have the company of their mothers they fail to develop normal patterns of social behaviour, and any contact with peers tends to be of an anti-social nature. We can therefore conclude that throughout life friendships provide a context for social and emotional growth (Van Lieshout & Doise, 1998) and offer security and support in times of stress. However, Maccoby (1980) believes that there are different socialisation processes for girls and boys and that female-only friendships facilitate interpersonal skills and have a socio-emotional focus, with the provision for giving and taking support, while male friendships are more orientated towards individual factors such as achievement and competitiveness.

It is beyond the scope of this section to discuss this here but bullying is a source of social influence that may have a significant and often negative effect on development.

In adolescence peers provide the main source of support. Buhrmester (1996) found that intimate self-disclosure is most likely to be made to a friend by the age of 15 years.

Play

The role of play is a fundamental factor/social influence on development as it not only gives the child an opportunity to interact with peers but will also allow them to experience aspects of the social world in a hypothetical way. Symbolic play (play where objects act as 'symbols' of something in the real world) does not generally emerge until about 12–18 months, and even then it is the child itself who is still the 'agent' although this rapidly transfers to being able to use toys for such purposes. True pretend play does not generally emerge until approximately the second year. Games also contribute to a child's ability to show moral reasoning since they provide rules that aid the understanding of social order. According to Verenikina, Harris and Lysaght (2003) the most significant psychological achievements of early childhood occur while children engage in play.

> *It is often hard to separate the impact of each of these types of social influences on development since there is not always a clear division. For example, play aids development but needs to be initiated and encouraged by the mother and additionally encompasses peers – thus emphasing the dual role of all these aspects.*

Key thinkers

Baumrind (1967, 1971, 1977) (in D.R. Shaffer, 1993: 571–572)

Looked at the effects of parental control/child-rearing style on development. Parents and children were observed and parents interviewed, and Baumrind established three types of parental control. The box below outlines the characteristics of these styles and the effects on the child's development.

Parental style	Effect on development
Authoritarian Restrictive parenting which expects obedience to set rules.	Child is: Fearful, unhappy, hostile, unfriendly and vulnerable. Overall, child is *conflicted-irritable*
Authoritative Restrictions are imposed and child is expected to obey them but these are explained and meaningful. Parents are responsive to child's needs.	Child is: Self-reliant and co-operative, friendly and cheerful. Curious and achievement orientated. Overall child is *energetic-friendly*

(Cont'd)

Permissive Freedom of expression and behaviour is permitted with few demands or rules imposed on the child.	Child is: Rebellious, impulsive and aggressive and low in achievement and self control. Overall child is *impulsive-aggressive.*

Hinde (1987)

Argued that interaction with peers increases in complexity and the nature of social interaction, and that this occurs in three successive stages:

- Interactions – which are the result of a two-way process where there is engagement in activities at a similar level.
- Relationships – are dependent on interactions but entail a sense of more serious commitment.
- Groups – exist at a wider level and facilitate cohesiveness and sense of hierarchy, in other words a sense of inclusion and order.

Bigelow (1977) (in D.R. Shaffer, 1993: 629)

Found that children's expectations about friendships progress through three stages:

- Reward–cost stage – friendship is based on similar activities and mutual benefits.
- Normative stage – shared rules and values become important and a sense of co-operation develops.
- Empathic stage – intimacy and self-disclosure become important.

Piaget (1962)

Was a fundamental theorist in determining that the interactions that play provides are a key factor in promoting role-taking behaviour and allowing children to both experience, and practise skills which will contribute to their social perspective-taking as well as their interpersonal understanding. Piaget claimed that symbolic play can be divided into two key stages:

Stage 1: 0–4 years

- Familiar actions are applied to new objects, although such play is still fundamentally based on the role the object plays in real life.
- Schemas or blocks of knowledge about the world are transferred from/ imitated from the child's observation of others and thus the child may use objects in an imaginative or imitative way.
- Real scenes can be replaced by imaginative ones and over time imaginary play may predominate, involving both scenes and people – thus complex symbols are now combined.

Stage 2: 4–7 years

Play becomes more structured and the child will enforce rules that help imitate and construct a sense of reality, with peers interacting in a way that also resembles real social interactions. Thus play becomes less random both in terms of playing with rather than around others, and in its organisation.

Vygotsky (1978)

Believed that play creates a broad zone of proximal development (the difference between a child's actual and potential levels of development) both in cognitive and socio-emotional development, because in imaginative play children practise their cognitive abilities and the rules they encounter in the social world. They can find out about social roles and the rules of society. And may do so in a way that is more advanced than those skills they use on an everyday basis. Thus separation of thought from actions and objects, the development of mental representation and symbolic function of play is important (Verenikina, Harris & Lysaght, 2003). Vygotsky further argued that make-believe play is socially and culturally determined, and therefore play further allows children to acquire the tools and meanings of their culture.

Parten (1932, 1933) (in Dockett and Fleer 1999: 61–62)

Described a number of social categories of play:

- onlooker – a child observes play of others
- solitary play
- parallel play – when children play alongside one another but where there is little interaction among them
- group play – where children actually play together, doing similar things and co-ordinating their actions

> ### REMEMBER

Social influences in development

➤ Parents influence virtually every aspect of development. They are crucial initially for determining the type of attachment the child has, which then contributes to the child's sense of safety and exploration of the world as well as their own internal working model of themselves.

➤ Peers act as reinforcing agents, as role models and objects for social comparison, and provide a safe base from which new ideas and behaviours can be tested. As such, they are critical for social and personality development as they help the child acquire new skills and provide a context for social and emotional growth.

➤ The role of play is a fundamental factor/social influence on development as it not only gives the child an opportunity to interact with its peers but will also allow them to experience aspects of the social world in a hypothetical way.

Handy Hints for evaluating work of key thinkers

• Harris (2000) in Harris & Butterworth (2004: 215) states that 'pretend play is not an early distortion of the real world but an initial exploration of possible worlds', thus criticising the view Piaget postulated.

• Parten was criticised for underestimating the ability of young children to engage in social levels of play; the role of individual ways of engagement in play should not be overlooked (Verenikina, Harris & Lysaght, 2003).

• Operationalisation of interactions in childhood, for example stages of peer relationships, is difficult and much of the work is based on observational techniques which may contain bias and lack true experimenter control.

• Not only do parents influence the development of their child, but this is a reciprocal relationship so the child may also influence the development of the parents' child-rearing styles.

Tasks

1 Design a play activity suitable for preschoolers which would encourage their social development. Justify your choice of activity using your knowledge of psychological theory.

2 Choose a couple of friends from infant/junior school, from senior school and from university. Write down their names and then

brainstorm the reasons for your friendships – consider similarities, shared interests, etc. Now write down what you have gained from each friendship at that stage of your life and what you have contributed. Write up a summary piece on how peers have therefore contributed to your personal development. How does this relate to the research evidence provided in this section/your textbooks.

3 Using your textbooks, compile research on the specific effects parents have on development. Look up at least one research study on their influence on social development, cognitive development, moral development and one specialised area, for example antisocial behaviour or psychological disorder.

Essay questions

"Discuss the role of parents and peers on development"

Any introductory paragraph to this essay would benefit from defining the process of socialisation and the contribution that parents and peers can make to the various aspects of development, including cognitive, social, moral and emotional. In order to show yourself a true developmental psychologist, however, you will then need to narrow down your focus and look at specific areas of research. In each case you must outline the relevant research and, more importantly, highlight the contribution it makes to development – for example, how parental styles influence personality. In order to complete an essay that shows up-to-date research you will need to have carried out Task 3. Remember that in order to show a balanced view, however, you will also need to highlight the difficulties in assuming any relationship from such research, including the methods of study used and the other factors (such as nature) that might contribute to development. Only by doing this is it possible to draw any conclusions about the role parents and peers play in development.

"Outline and evaluate theories of play"

Various theories of play are relevant to this title, particularly Piaget's and Vygotsky's. You will need to begin by looking at their definitions in detail and then proceed to show how such theories contribute to development at each of the

*various stages. This will include the learning of rules, social skills and moral rea-
soning. The overriding factor must be that play is a fundamental factor/social
influence on development, as it not only gives the child an opportunity to interact
with its peers but will also allow it to experience aspects of the social world in a
hypothetical way. This conclusion must also, however, be evaluated and any
notes of caution about these theories of play discussed before overall conclusions can be drawn.*

Common Pitfalls

- *A common mistake students make is to assume that each of these areas is distinct.
  In fact it is often hard to separate the impact of each of these types of social
  influences on development, since there is not always a clear division.*
- *It is too simplistic to assume that parents' child-rearing practice/social influence will
  determine their development, as many other factors are involved – as can be seen in
  this section. Notice must also be taken of class bias, where assumptions are made
  about the middle classes being more competent or better at facilitating a child's
  development.*
- *To avoid an ethnocentric view on development it is worth bearing in mind that there
  are cross-cultural differences in the social influence that peers have on development,
  and indeed the role of parents and play.*

Textbook Guide

MACCOBY, E. E. (1980). *Social development: psychological growth and the
parent–child relationship.* New York: Harcourt Brace Jovanovich. This covers the
area of sociability and chapter one is of particular relevance. It gives a good
overview of the field.

SCHAFFER, D. R. AND EMERSON, P.E. (1980). *Social development: An introduction.*
Blackwell. This text gives the key ideas and evidence on a child's social development, providing a sound basis from which to study this topic, including
answers to practical questions and a good review of research.

www.vtaide.com/png/social.htm
Links to relevant and up-to-date articles on social development of children.

2.8

development of self and identity

Core areas

- Development of competent self
- Development of self-esteem
- Development of social self
- Erikson (1963) – stages of identity formation
- Looking-glass self
- Marcia's theory of adolescent development
- Piaget
- Public versus private self
- Rouge test
- Stages of identity formation
- Stages of impression formation
- Stages of social perspective taking

Learning outcomes

By the end of this section you should be able to:

- understand that there are different types of self;
- outline the stages involved in the development of the self;
- define the concept of self-esteem, the scales used to look at this and summarise the main findings in this area;
- indicate what the rouge test is and how it helps the identification of self-recognition;
- describe and evaluate Marcia's ideas on identity development in adolescence;
- outline the stages of impression formation, stages of social perspective taking, and the development of the social and the competent self.

Running themes

- Behaviourism
- Cognitive-developmental viewpoint
- Informational-processing approach
- Nature
- Nurture

- Stage theory of development
- Transformational change

Introduction

Cooley (1902) and Mead (1934) believed we have a 'looking-glass self'. They believed that our sense of identity is simply a reflection of how we believe other people see us and indeed how other people respond.

> *Self-concept is partly a social construction. Thus children are born as a blank slate without a sense of self.*

A summary of the main findings in relation to the stages of identity formation/development of self is outlined below:

- *1–4 months* – primary circular reactions are displayed, that is, the sense of self is focused on pleasure in body functions/movements.
- *3–6 months* – there is recognition of self as independent of caregiver, although some believe this occurs earlier.
- *4–8 months* – secondary circular reactions occur, namely repetition of actions that interact with the environment and are external to the self.
- *18–24 months* old – the child shows self-recognition when the rouge test is applied. The categorical self, where one's age, size, gender, beliefs, values and preferred activities are identified, emerges at about the same time.
- *2–3 years* – a struggle for independence and autonomy emerges.
- *3–5 years* – most 3–5-year-olds are able to discriminate between the public versus the private self. According to D.R. Shaffer (1993: 437), the public self contains 'those aspects of self that others can see or infer' but the private self is 'those inner, or subjective, aspects of self that are known only to the individual and are not available for public scrutiny'.
- *4–5 years* – autonomy is displayed, new skills acquired and pride achieved in their attainment.
- *7–10 years* – when describing self and others there is less reliance on possessions and physical attributes and acknowledgement of psychological characteristics of self and others.
- *8 years* – a distinction is made between inner states and outward appearances (Selman, 1980).
- *9–10 years* – the focus of self extends to categorical information such as age, name, gender, address and physical characteristics and preferred activities.
- *11–12 years* – the focus of self also extends to traits, beliefs, motivations and interpersonal relations.

Key thinkers

Harter (1982) – development of self-esteem

Self-esteem relates to 'a person's feelings about the qualities and characteristics that make up his or her self concept' (D.R. Shaffer, 1993: 439). She developed a scale consisting of 28 items which asks the child to evaluate how competent they are in four different areas – cognitive competence, social competence, physical competence and their general sense of self-worth. The scale was completed by 2097 8–9-year-old participants, and their teachers. Results indicated that the students own perception was indeed closely related to that of their teacher or peers and that they had clear ideas about whether they were indeed competent or not in each different area.

Lewis and Brooks-Gunn (1979) – rouge test

One way of assessing the development of self is to apply a spot of rouge to the face of a child and then place them in front of a mirror. If the child tries to rub it off themselves rather than the reflection, it can be assumed that they have acquired a sense of self-recognition. When the researchers tested 9–24-month-olds it was found that although a few 15–17-month-old children could do this, most did not do so until they were somewhere between 18 and 24 months old.

Erikson (1963) – stages of identity formation

- *2–3 years* – a struggle for independence and autonomy emerges.
- *4–5 years* – autonomy is displayed, new skills are being acquired and pride achieved in their attainment.
- *6–12-year-olds* – experience an industry versus inferiority crisis – measurement of self against peers is part of this stage.
- *12–15-year-olds* – identity crisis – no longer sure who they are and therefore self-esteem declines while they try to determine this.

Marcia (1966) – adolescents experience four different stages in identity formation

These include identity diffusion/confusion, identity foreclosure, identity moratorium and identity achievement. The adolescent therefore moves from not thinking about the issues, prematurely forming an opinion, the trying out of various possibilities and then to achieving their own identity as a result of these processes.

Barenboim (1981) – developmental stages of impression formation

When a sample was asked to describe three people whom they knew well, the following stages emerged:

1 Behavioural comparisons phase – behaviours are compared to give a sense of self and define others (6–8 years).

2 Psychological constructs phase – stable traits of self and others are now considered (8–9 to 10–11 years).

3 Psychological comparisons phase – a process of comparing and contrasting takes place (12–16 years).

Piaget (1965) – concept of self depends on cognitive development stages

- Pre-operational stage – self and others seen according to observable characteristics, actions and so on. World is seen only from one's own viewpoint (egocentrism).
- Concrete-operational stage (7–10 years) – as egocentrism declines, classification takes place and consistencies are perceived despite changes in appearance.
- Formal operations (11–12 years) – logical and systematic decisions about the traits of self and others become possible.

Selman (1980) – stages of social perspective taking

According to Selman a sense of self and identity can only develop once a child understands others and can discriminate between different perspectives. He proposed five different stages:

1 Egocentric or undifferentiated perspective (3–6 years) – children are unaware of any perspective except their own.

2 Social-informational role taking (6–8 years) – different perspectives are acknowledged but the child believes any different perspective held by others is due to their misinformation.

3 Self-reflective role taking (8–10 years) – there is recognition of different views but only alongside one's own and not simultaneously.

4 Mutual role taking (10–12 years) – empathy develops and thus viewpoints can be simultaneously experienced before a response is made.

5 Social and conventional system role taking (12–15 years+) – perspectives are looked at within the social context.

REMEMBER

> ➤ Students' own perception of self appears to be closely related to that of their teacher or peers and they tend to have clear ideas about whether they are competent in various areas.
> ➤ Most children recognise self using the rouge test somewhere between 18–24 months old.
> ➤ Erikson believed that identity occurs in various stages which range from trying to establish autonomy to experiencing an identity crisis.
> ➤ Impression formation involves a behavioural comparisons phase (6–8 years), a psychological constructs phase (8–9 to 10–11 years) and a psychological comparisons phase (12–16 years).
> ➤ According to Piaget, self develops in conjunction with a developing cognitive maturity throughout the pre-operational, concrete operational and formal operational stages.
> ➤ According to Selman, a sense of self and identity can only develop once a child understands others and can discriminate between different perspectives.

Development of social self

D.R. Shaffer (1993: 449) defined sociability as the 'willingness to interact with others and to seek their attention and approval'.

This is important in the development of self, as we have seen that this is partly derived from the social interactions and responses of others.

From birth, infants display behaviours, such as smiling, that are inherently sociable as they attempt to establish attachment. It is also generally accepted that they prefer the company of humans to non-social stimuli (see section 2.10). Mueller and Vandell (1979) propose that three stages of sociability occur in the first two years of life: at first the infant is object-centred, then begins a simple interactive phase but by 18 months it shows clear social interaction and exchanges in the complementary interactive phase.

There are, however, individual differences in the development of sociability. Some believe that this is due to genetic factors, others that it is due to the quality of attachment, with secure infants being more inherently sociable (using Ainsworth and Bell's criteria (1970) – see section 2.10) and another perspective (the 'ordinal position hypothesis' – Schacter, 1959) viewing it as a factor of birth order with first-borns displaying greater sociability towards adults than towards peers.

During the preschool period sociability develops further, with social gestures directed towards more sources – peers, teachers, and so on. Research indicates that sociability then becomes a fairly stable attribute from about 2 years old (see, for example, Bronson, 1985).

Development of a sense of achievement/the competent self

White (1959) believes children have a basic and inbuilt/intrinsic need to master their environment and the people in it (effectance motivation).

One of the most famous theories of motivation is McClelland et al's (1953) theory on the need for achievement which suggests that is a learned concept where one needs to achieve success and seek evaluation based on this. Harter (1981) believes children may attempt to achieve for one of two reasons: either to satisfy their own needs for mastery (intrinsic orientation) or for external rewards (extrinsic orientation). Again, home environment and attachment have been correlated with the development of the competent self, with securely attached and appropriately stimulated infants most likely to develop happily in this area.

Related to this sense of self, however, is a child's locus of control – that is the extent to which they either believe that their behaviour will influence an outcome (internal locus of control) or that it will in fact be determined by the environment (external locus of control). (See Rotter, 1966 for a discussion of locus of control). Logically it can be assumed that children who have an internal locus of control will be more likely to achieve a competent self, as they feel they apply themselves to obtain the desired outcome. Previous experiences of success or failure will however influence the development of locus of control since Weiner's (1986) attribution theory predicts that attributions made for experiences of success and failure were made based on three areas. Firstly, a locus which could be internal or external (see Rotter above); secondly, stability, that is, whether the cause is stable or changes over time; and lastly control-lability. Thus a child who has an internal locus of control which is stable and controllable is able to obtain a sense of the self as competent. In the absence of this, experiences of failure may lead to learned help-lessness (Seligman, 1975).

Handy Hints for evaluating work on the development of self/identity

- There are differing viewpoints in this area that you need to be aware of, some focused more on learning, others on innate abilities and some on the role of cognitive development.
- You need to be aware, however, that these are all guidelines and are not absolute, as the role of individual differences must be accounted for.
- The self is difficult to test empirically, and this must be taken into account when evaluating the theories.

Tasks

1 Look at Marcia's theory in your textbook. Using her criteria can you identify which stage of identity formation you are in? Justify your answer. What were the difficulties of making this decision?

2 Work within small groups (no more than four). First, write down five words you would use to describe yourself. Now ask each of the others in your group to write down five words about you. Is there a comparison? Many of the theories of self predict that our own sense of self is partly reflected from the way others experience us – have you found this to be the case? Is there common ground between what you have written and that of your peers?

3 Carry out the rouge test on a young child. Does what you find correlate with that of the researchers? Were there any problems in carrying out this study or any issues you felt you needed to be aware of?

Essay questions

❝What does psychological theory have to say about the development of the self?❞

This is a broad question that allows you to cover a range of material. You will need to start by clearly defining the various aspects of the self and give a summary of the main findings in this area as a general introduction. It will then be necessary to become more focused, for example by taking the key thinkers, expanding on the work they carried out and then referring back to the question, stating what their work tells us about the development of self. Do not forget, however, that each theory will need to be evaluated; as a developmental psychologist it is of importance that you show a critical awareness of the usefulness of any theory. Some reference, applying this same structure, will also need to be made to the development of the social and the competent self.

Common Pitfalls

- There are many terms associated with this section and you must make sure that you are aware of the differences between them – for example, of the difference between self-identity and self-esteem.
- There is also deemed to be more than one type of self and too often students lump all types together under the heading 'self'. It is therefore important to know when it is appropriate to do so and when you will need to make divisions.
- Failure to understand that all of these theories are just guidelines and not prescriptive and that there will always be individual differences will aid your evaluation and thoughts on these topics.

Textbook Guide

BENNETT, M., & SANI, F. (2003). *Development of the social self.* Psychology Press: Taylor & Francis group. Using a social identity theory perspective this text examines the acquisition and development of children's self-identity.

ERIKSON, E. H. (1968). *Identity: youth and crisis.* New York: Norton. A look at the complexity and trials of social identity stages in the lifespan.

HARTER, S. (2001). *Construction of self: a developmental perspective.* Guildford publications. A research-based text that looks at self-development and self-representations.

2.9	
gender development	

Core areas

- Biosocial theory
- Cognitive-developmental theory
- Electra complex
- Gender consistency
- Gender identity
- Gender schema theory
- Gender stability
- Oedipus conflict
- Psychoanalytic theory
- Sociobiological theory
- Social learning theory

Learning outcomes

By the end of this section you should be able to:

- define and understand the key concepts above;
- describe each of the explanations offered for gender development;
- show an understanding of whether they are psychological or biological theories, or both;
- evaluate the theories in terms of the research evidence available to support them;
- understand the limitations of each approach.

Running themes

- Cognitive-developmental viewpoint
- Nature
- Nurture
- Psychoanalytic viewpoint
- Stage theory of development
- Transformational change

Introduction

Gender itself refers to the psychological characteristics associated with being male or female. Gender identity goes beyond the biological aspects focusing on the awareness of being male or female and will include aspects of gender role (expectations about gender-appropriate behaviours) based partially on stereotypes. It is the first step in the development of the child's self-concept as it helps it label itself according to gender and therefore start to label others in a similar way.

> As we shall see throughout this section gender may be the result of both nature and nurture.

Key thinkers/theories

Freud (1938) – psychoanalytic theory

Freud believed gender identity is acquired through identification with the same-sex parent. According to Freud, boys develop an Oedipal complex by which they experience sexual desire for their mother but because they fear that their father will find out about this and castrate them, they instead try to identify with their father to avoid discovery. Thus, resolution of the Oedipus conflict, in part, involves gender identity, adopted from the example set by the father. For girls identification with the mother derives from a similar process but instead of the fear of castration girls experience the Electra complex, identifying with the mother for fear of her finding out that she actually feels penis envy towards the father. Thus, these identification processes in the phallic stage of development (3–6 years) play a major role in the development of gender stereotypes.

Kohlberg (1966) – cognitive-developmental theory

Kohlberg proposed a stage theory of gender identity and gender role development, proposing that as cognition matures so does the child's understanding of gender. This means children can only acquire gender concepts when they have reached an appropriate age and are 'ready' to acquire this knowledge. When children have acquired a gender concept this leads them to identify with members of the same gender and actively seek information about gender-appropriate behaviour (and therefore future gender development). The specific stages he has identified include gender identity (2–3 years) where the child recognises their gender, the gender stability stage (3–7 years) where the child accepts that gender is fixed, and lastly gender consistency (7–12 years) where the child recognises that gender will not change despite behaviours.

Martin and Halverson (1983) – gender schema theory

Gender schema begin to form as soon as the child recognises that there is a difference between males and females (the term schema means 'concept clusters' that a child acquires in relation to gender, such as gender stereotypes). Children develop schemas or 'theories' about gender-appropriate behaviour, which help them to organise and interpret their experience, the readiness to categorises gender information driving the development of gender. So the fundamental theory is that gender stereotypes come before the child acquires a gender concept.

Bandura (1977) – social learning theory

Children learn gender-appropriate behaviour through the application of reward and punishment, or vicarious learning (observation). These behaviours may be reinforced unconsciously either directly or indirectly by observing stereotypes, for example, by observing people being rewarded or punished for their feminine or masculine activity and this may occur through observing the media, books, peers, and so on.

Money and Ehrhardt (1972) – biosocial theory

There are a number of biological factors that initially determine gender, including inheritance from the father of either the X or Y chromosome and the subsequent hormone production in this neonatal stage. They believed that after birth, however, the child would adopt the identity given to them by other social agents in response to their physical appearance/genitalia. As the child becomes aware of this, a basic gender identity is formed. Thus the model specifically combines biological development with the social processes that lead to gender development.

Sociobiological theory

Purely a biological theory, this states that gender arises because of the genes passed on through evolution and thus males and females behave and look different because it is adaptive; these differences maximise reproduction and ensure survival of the genes.

Handy Hints for evaluating theories of gender development

- When Smith and Lloyd (1978) presented women playing with a baby who was dressed in either blue or pink they found that they would give them the 'gender-appropriate' toys to play with, for example, those in blue were given a hammer and those in pink a doll, supporting the idea that gender stereotypes are reinforced and learnt from as early as 4 months old.

- Social learning accounts fail to explain how and why gender changes over time and it is too simplistic to say that a child's gender is passively shaped in this way. Additionally, Jacklin and Maccoby (1978) believe children are not actually treated as differently as the theory portrays.
- Slabey and Frey (1975) asked preschool children some questions including: 'Are you a boy or girl?' 'Were you a boy or girl when you were a baby?' and 'When you grow up will you be a mummy or a daddy?' The results demonstrated the three stages of cognitive development outlined by Kohlberg as the children showed recognition of their gender from a young age, and that it had not changed and would not change.
- The focus of the cognitive-developmental theory is too narrow, ignoring biological factors, emotion and the social environment.
- Liben and Signorella (1993) showed children pictures of adults in opposite gender activities and found that because they had not yet reached the appropriate stage of cognitive development such adults were ignored, supporting the idea that children can only acknowledge gender stereotypes that are consistent with their stage of development.
- Overall, however, there are only weak associations between gender awareness and actual behaviour.
- Biological theories do account for the physical aspect of gender but ignore the psychological and social aspects that interact with this.

REMEMBER

Theories of gender development
Gender may develop because of:

➢ Identification with the same-sex parent due to the Oedipal or Electra complexes that occur in the phallic stage of development (3–6 years).

➢ As cognition matures so does the child's understanding of gender.

➢ The child's recognition that there is a difference between males and females helps them develop schemas or 'theories' about gender-appropriate behaviour, reward and punishment, or vicarious learning (observation).

➢ Biological factors and the contribution of social factors that result from interpretations of this.

➢ The genes passed on through evolution cause males and females to behave differently and look different, because it is adaptive, and these differences maximise reproduction and ensure survival of the genes.

Tasks

1 Carry out an internet search on the case of David Reimer who was originally the focus of the psychologist Money, and who was used to support his sociobiological theory. Write up a brief synopsis of this case study and then provide an argument as to why this actually contradicts this theory of gender development.

2 To consolidate your understanding make a list of theories that indicate gender development is biological, those that suggest it is psychological, or both.

3 Complete Table 3 on theories of gender development, including the research evidence to support them and the criticisms of such theories. You will need to use your textbooks for extra reading in order to do this.

Essay questions

"Outline and evaluate two or more theories of gender development"

It is important here to decide in advance which theories you feel would best cover this topic – choosing the biosocial and sociobiological theories, for example, would not give you much scope for discussion. You would benefit from a range of different perspectives to allow you to gain your evaluation marks. You will need to begin by making it clear which theories you are focusing on. A succinct description is also vital – one that covers the key concepts presented by the theory. Since you are, however, required to be psychologists you should than evaluate these in terms of the contribution they make to psychology. For example, is there any research evidence to support the concept of gender development and if so what is it? How does it support the theory? A similar principle then needs to be applied to the criticisms of the theories – what are their limitations? The key skill that you are therefore required to demonstrate is that you can take an overall perspective about gender development informed by the research evidence presented to you.

"Discuss the extent to which gender development can be viewed as a psychological process"

This section has presented many different viewpoints concerning gender development, some of which argue that it is a psychological concept and others which make more of the biological input. The title lends itself to your addressing the psychological perspectives first, but remember it is not simply asking for a description of these theories. Like any psychological essay it wants you to demonstrate an ability to weigh up two sides of any argument, and you will therefore need to progress to those that have a biological input to indicate that although gender might be a psychological construct this may not be entirely the case. By covering both perspectives you can therefore conclude the actual extent to which it is psychological.

Common Pitfalls

- *Be sure that you understand which concepts/definitions belong in which theory because it is easy to confuse them when dealing with the gender topic as a whole.*
- *You must also ensure that you understand which theories focus on nurture, and which on nature – that is, which ones see it as a learned concept and which ones see it as a product of biology/inheritance.*
- *Knowing the theories will not gain you access to the higher marks, you need to go beyond this and look at the research to support the theories of gender development and the limitations associated with each of the approaches.*

Textbook Guide

GOLOMBOK, S. (1994). *Gender development*. Cambridge: Cambridge University Press. This provides a general introduction to the topic including definitions and measurement. It also goes on to look at gender stereotypes, prenatal influences and many of the key theories, including the psychoanalytic approach, cognitive development, schemas and the role of play, intimate relationships, families, school work and emotions. It will therefore also provide extension reading around this topic.

MARTIN, C. L., & HALVERSON, C. F. (1983). The effects of sex-typing schemas on young children's memory. *Child development*, 54, 563–574. This provides a more detailed insight into gender schema theory.

SMITH, P. K., COWIE, H., & BLADES, M. (2003). *Understanding children's development* (4th ed.). Blackwell. Part Two (chapter 6) provides a comprehensive guide to the development of gender identity in the section on becoming socially aware.

Table 3 Gender Development

Theory	Description	Supporting Research	Criticisms
Psychoanalytic			
Cognitive-developmental			
Gender schema			
Social learning			
Biosocial			
Sociobiology			

2.10

emotional development, deprivation and enrichment

Core areas

- Affectional bond
- Affectionless psychopathy
- Attachment
- Bowlby's theory of attachment
- Cognitive-developmental theory of attachment
- Critical versus sensitive period
- Deprivation
- Emotion
- Enrichment
- Ethology
- Imprinting
- Indiscriminate attachment phase
- Individual differences and attachment
- Insecure avoidant attachment
- Insecure resistant attachment
- Interactional synchrony
- Learning theory of attachment
- Maternal deprivation hypothesis
- Monotropy
- Multiple attachment
- Object permanence
- Preattachment phase
- Privation
- Secure attachment
- Specific attachment
- Stages of attachment
- Strange situation

Learning outcomes

By the end of this section you should be able to:

- define the key terms outlined above;
- define the key stages involved in emotional development;

- understand that attachment is a key area in such development;
- define the different types, stages and theories of attachment and the individual differences in attachment;
- outline the short- and long-term effects of deprivation including the research evidence on which this is based, and be able to evaluate this work;
- examine the effects of privation and the studies that support this;
- acknowledge the work of enrichment programmes in emotional development.

Running themes

- Behaviourism
- Cognitive-developmental viewpoint
- Ecological validity
- Ethics
- Ethology
- Nature
- Nurture
- Psychoanalytic viewpoint
- Stage theory of development.

Introduction

Emotional understanding in infancy is a complex process involving the understanding not only of the child's own emotions but also of those of others, including both the recognition of feelings and the expression of them. Preschool children use emotional labels but by the school years they are better able to distinguish between internal feelings and expression of emotion with more conscious awareness of their own emotional expressions.

Izard (1982) carried out a number of experiments and found that different emotions appear at various times over the first two years of life.

An approximate time-line would look something like this:

- *1 month* – infants are capable of displaying five primary emotions – interest, surprise, joy, anger and fear (Johnson et al., 1982).
- *3–4 months* – anger and sadness appear and children become capable of distinguishing between emotions in photos of faces. Mother's expression and voice are recognisable.
- *5–7 months* – fear, shame and shyness appear.

- *7–10 months* – the infant becomes better at interpreting emotional expression, and thus social referencing takes place (being able to interpret someone else's emotions before deciding one's own emotional expression).
- *12 months+* – guilt and contentment are shown.
- *18–24 months* – the child can now talk about these emotional feelings.

The display of emotion is a two-way process with the mother. Klaus and Kennell (1976) looked at the emotional bonding between mother and neonate. Skin-to-skin contact was seen to be of key importance and mothers who had more such contact with their new baby had children who were happier and better physically and mentally developed than their peers. Timing of the contact was the most important factor – especially in the first 6–12 hours, which is therefore seen as a sensitive period.

Attachment

Maccoby (1980) defined an attachment as 'a relatively enduring emotional tie to a specific other person'.

> So, attachment is used to describe a special kind of relationship between two people. It can be referred to as a type of 'affectional bond', by which the baby seeks closeness to someone.

As an attachment depends on an interaction between two people it is only by looking at the behaviours of the infant/caregiver that we are able to see if an attachment exists.

> Maccoby (1980) identified four behaviours that may allow us to identify an attachment:

1 Trying to get close to the caregiver (especially in times of stress).

2 Showing distress when separated from the caregiver.

3 Showing pleasure when reunited.

4 Generally orientating behaviour towards the caregiver.

Attachment is therefore a special emotional bond between a child and its caregiver/s. Some believe this occurs with just one person/the mother (a monotrophic bond) and others believe that multiple attachments are possible. There are two specific types of attachment – a secure attachment where a baby shows some distress when separated from its caregiver but is able to continue to play and is readily comforted upon the caregiver's return. Insecure attachments occur when the child displays resistant or avoidant behaviour following separation from the caregiver. A secure attachment provides the child with a stable and secure base from which to explore the world, and is believed to be as important for emotional development as vitamins and proteins are for physical development.

Deprivation occurs when the bond between a mother and child is broken in some way but privation is when the child has never had the opportunity to establish an attachment with an appropriate caregiver (for example if they are orphaned) – unlike deprivation they have not lost the attachment but have never formed it in the beginning.

Theories of attachment

Cognitive-developmental theory

Attachment depends on intellectual development. The infant must be capable, at a cognitive level, of distinguishing between familiar and unfamiliar people and recognising that key attachment figures are permanent even in their absence (object permanence).

Ethology

Attachments are biological. We are born with 'signals' that have evolved to encourage attachment, so it is an evolutionary process that ensures survival. It is an instinct, and Lorenz (1937) found that animals will 'imprint' (follow the attachment object instinctively from birth) during a critical period, and that this is automatic and irreversible.

Learning theory

Attachment is a *learned process* (due to nurture). Infants attach because of classical conditioning – they attach to the mother because she is associated with providing food and attention. So the infant learns to attach to this person based on the associations that are made. Learning theory suggests that a child learns to form an attachment because they experience a desire for food as soon as they are born. They have a need to reduce the drive state (so, to be fed). This is a primary drive because it is innate and arises from a biological need. The child therefore soon learns that food is a reward (it stops them being hungry). This is called a primary reinforcer. Quickly the mother becomes a secondary reinforcer because the child associates her with the food. However, the mother also offers security and contact comfort. She is warm, sensitive and responsive and therefore a secondary drive is created, by which the child seeks the mother because she is comforting. Attachment is a two-way process because when the child also responds to the mother (for example 'coo', smiling) the mother will seek repeated interaction, often during the feeding process, in the first stage of a child's life.

Bowlby's theory

The adult/caregiver is genetically programmed to form an attachment with the infant in order to protect it. Attachment gives the child the opportunity to be around adults and therefore provides a safe base from which the infant can explore the world. The attachment develops between the infant and caregiver because the infant displays 'social releasers' – these are behaviours that elicit/produce a reaction from the caregiver, and include crying, smiling, etc. Attachment is a biological (innate) process and there is a *critical period* of development. This means that if the attachment is not formed within the first 2.5 years it will not occur at all. A 'monotrophic bond' is formed – that is a special bond with just one other person. The mother is therefore unique. Bowlby believes that if this bond is not formed, or is broken, then there will be permanent emotional damage because children only develop socially and emotionally when an attachment provides them with feelings of security. High self-esteem and emotional and social development are therefore derived from having a sensitive, emotionally responsive and supportive caregiver with whom the child has developed an attachment (the internal working model). If the child does not have an attachment then they will not develop emotionally (maternal deprivation hypothesis). Affectionless psychopathy may result, where there is a lack of emotional development, a lack of concern for others, a lack of guilt and an inability to form lasting relationships.

> ### *REMEMBER*
>
> **Theories of attachment**
> Attachment can be the result of:
>
> ➤ maturing cognitions
> ➤ an evolutionary and instinctive process
> ➤ an innate need to form a monotrophic bond
> ➤ learning that it brings satisfaction and comfort

Handy Hints for evaluating theories of attachment

- Harlow and Zimmerman (1959) – provided young monkeys with two wire 'mothers'. One of these 'mothers' had a feeding bottle which could be used to feed the infant, the other 'mother' was covered in soft cloth and offered 'contact comfort' (was comfortable to touch). The baby monkeys spent most of their time with the mother who was covered in material and not with the one that offered it food. This study therefore supports learning theory as it shows that the infant (monkey) will learn to go to the one that offers it the most comfort and that attachment is based on interaction, although we must be careful about generalising Harlow and Zimmerman's study to human behaviour because monkeys and children will not necessarily act in the same way.
- The behaviourist approach/learning theory can be criticised for being too *reductionist*, in that ideas about human behaviour are over-simplified. In terms of attachment it could therefore be argued that it is too simple to say that babies attach because of reinforcement, as attachment may also depend on a number of other (more complex) factors.
- It is difficult to separate attachment based on the biological need for food and attachment based on the attention given during the feeding process.
- Infants display more than one attachment so the concept of monotrophy can be criticised. Schaffer and Emerson's (1964) stages of attachment demonstrate that multiple attachments can be formed.
- The idea of a *critical period* has also been criticised. Instead a *sensitive period* has been suggested. This is where the child should ideally form an attachment in the first 2.5 years of life, but it can be formed later.
- Cupboard love theory rejects the idea that infants attach to those who are responsive and instead believes that love/attachment is based purely on a biological need for food.
- Hazan and Shaver (1987) examined whether attachment/lack of attachment does have an impact on later development as Bowlby's theory had suggested. To test this they were looking at the styles of adult romantic relationships and seeing if they could be related to early attachment experiences. A 'love quiz' was printed in a newspaper to assess early attachment experiences, later

experiences of adult romantic love and beliefs about romantic love. Respondents who were securely attached as infants had trusting and lasting relationships. Anxious/insecure infants worried that partners didn't love them, and avoidant/ insecure types feared intimacy and believed that they did not need love to be happy, which supports Bowlby's theory as it shows that early attachments do act as a template for the future (in this case in establishing adult relationships). However, the data is correlational – so it only assumes a relationship between two things and we cannot prove they are related. We therefore can't be certain that early attachment caused the later romantic style.

Key thinkers

Schaffer and Emerson (1964) – stages of attachment

Schaffer and Emerson believe that attachments form in stages. They aimed to discover whether babies do learn attachment behaviour and followed 60 Scottish infants for eighteen months, observing them every four weeks, and assessing them for separation and stranger anxiety. They found that attachment tends to form in stages: at 0–2 months they display pre-attachment behaviour showing similar responses to all objects; an indiscriminate attachment phase develops at 2–7 months, in which infants start to distinguish familiar and unfamiliar people; a specific attachment then develops at 7–24 months and this is marked by separation protest and stranger anxiety; and lastly multiple attachments are formed from 8 months onwards. The study further suggested that infants learn to attach to those who are most responsive and to those who offer a high level of stimulation.

Robertson and Robertson (1971)

Produced a series of films of children who were experiencing separation. They studied a number of children who had been placed in short term nursery/residential care (for example, 'John'). All of the children were experiencing short-term deprivation, usually due to the mother being admitted to hospital. The films were therefore case studies, as each child was recorded individually and their behaviour later coded by the psychologists. Evidence was found to support the protest–despair– detachment model. For example, when studying just one child – 'John' – it was found that he clearly showed each phase. Protest – he tried to make attachments with the adults in the nursery but they had little time to spend with him and he started to show signs of distress. Despair – he began to cry more, refused food, became demanding and had difficulties sleeping. He would be comforted by an adult but was unable to receive ongoing individual attention because of the nature of the nursery. He was therefore starting to show signs of despair. Detachment – after a period of time he started to show detachment – for example, gave up trying for attention and when the mother returned ignored her and refused to be comforted. It seems that even in the short term deprivation has an effect on a child and Robertson and Robertson concluded that it is therefore crucial that in any period of separation a child is provided with good substitute care that closely resembles the child's familiar routine.

Ainsworth and Bell (1970) – individual differences and attachment – the 'Strange Situation'

The authors devised a method for testing the type and security of attachments a child was experiencing. It is an experimental procedure, consisting of seven steps, which looks at the behaviour of the infant when separated from its mother (for example, how it reacts and whether it continues to play with toys), its behaviour in the presence of a stranger and its response upon the mother's return. Two specific areas are measured – a child's separation anxiety (how anxious does it become when the mother leaves it behind) and stranger anxiety (how does it respond to a stranger when left alone with them). From this Ainsworth believed you could categorise a child's attachment behaviour as either secure (distress is shown on separation, but upon reunion with the mother behaviour returns to normal and the mother's company is preferred to that of a stranger) or insecure. If the child shows a resistant attachment type they are distressed upon separation but when the mother returns resist efforts to comfort them and are wary of the stranger. In contrast an anxious child does not react to either the mother leaving or returning and equally avoids the stranger.

Bowlby (1944) – maternal deprivation and the 44 thieves study

Bowlby's theory of attachment is outlined above. Critical to his claims was his original study which aimed to see if there was a relationship between maternal deprivation and later emotional problems. He studied 88 children from the clinic where he worked. Of that number, 44 were thieves referred for stealing and 44 were controls who had other emotional problems. The data were based on individual case studies and retrospective reports. So, each child and their past history were examined to see if there had been maternal separation/later emotional problems. Of the thieves 32 per cent were 'affectionless psychopaths' (see below). Of these, 86 per cent had experienced maternal deprivation before 5 years old. None of the controls was diagnosed as a psychopath and only 17 per cent had suffered deprivation. He therefore concluded that maternal deprivation causes emotional damage. It leads to affectionless psychopathy – a failure of emotional development, where there is a lack of concern for others, a lack of guilt and an inability to form lasting relationships.

Hodges and Tizard (1989)

These researchers examined the long-term effects of privation by studying a group of children who had experienced multiple caregivers until 2 years old, and then were adopted or restored to their biological parents (the children had not therefore had an opportunity to form an attachment). The sample consisted of 42 children. The children were originally followed up until the age of 8 and then, in 1989, Hodges and Tizard attempted to reassess them at 16 years old, making it therefore a longitudinal study. The children and their mothers or caregivers were interviewed and the interviews tape-recorded. Parents/care workers were also asked to complete a questionnaire rating the adolescent's behaviour, while the adolescent completed a questionnaire on social difficulty. A questionnaire was also sent to the student's school, focusing on relationships between teachers and peers. By age 8 most of the adopted children and some of the restored group had formed close attachments to their parents, despite the early lack of attachment in the institutions. According to parents the ex-institutional children did not present more problems than a comparison group, but their teachers believed they showed more attention-seeking behaviour, restlessness, disobedience and poor peer relationships, being seen as unpopular. At age 16 the restored groups still showed some difficulties. Both they, and their parents, were less likely to be attached to each other; they were rated less favourably than their siblings, were less affectionate, identified less with their parents and did not want to be involved in discussions. Both groups, however, showed similar relationships to adults and peers outside of the family. They sought more adult attention and approval, were more likely to have difficulties with their peer group, less likely to have a special friend or use peers for emotional support.

Handy Hints for evaluating the work of key thinkers

- The idea of stages suggests that early development is fixed at particular ages, but Schaffer and Emerson (1964) didn't account for the fact that every child is different and has varied experiences that will affect their stages of attachment.
- As the data collected was mainly based on observations by Schaffer and Emerson, the work could be biased as they might have simply found data to support what they were looking for (observer bias). Therefore, the results should be applied with caution.
- The children filmed by the Robertsons (1971) represent a very small sample and the findings cannot therefore be generalised to all children – others may behave differently when deprived for a short time. If they were aware that they were being observed/filmed then they may have not behaved naturally.
- Main and Solomon (1986) argue that the attachment categories in Ainsworth and Bell's study (1970) are too narrow, and that there is a fourth type of attachment called disorganised attachment, in which the child appears afraid of attachment figures and seeks very close contact with parents while at the same time trying to avoid it.
- The study has been criticised because it does not represent situations in real life where a baby and mother might be separated. It is therefore said to lack ecological validity and does not account for the differences in a child's background, and prior separation experiences. As such the Strange Situation cannot be used in all cultures because there are differences in child-rearing practices.
- The research in Bowlby's (1944) study is correlational so we can't *prove* that deprivation causes psychopathy. Other factors (for example, the environment) might have led to the stealing.
- It is also possible that the findings were biased. Bowlby expected to find evidence for deprivation and so his expectations led him to conclude that this caused the delinquency. To be truly fair he should have studied all children who had suffered early separation and not just those experiencing later problems.
- To be able to look fully at the effects of early privation the sample needs to be studied further; can, for example, the groups establish their own lasting relationships in life with a partner/children? They would need to be followed for 20 to 30 years to gain a more representative picture.
- One of the major problems with Hodges and Tizard's study (1989) was that not all of the children in the original sample could later be contacted. As we don't know how the early privation affected them, it is hard to generalise from the findings as they might be biased (for example, if those who were untraceable subsequently developed particularly well, or particularly badly, different conclusions might have been drawn).
- The children's own characteristics had not been taken into account and it is possible that those who were adopted in the beginning were simply 'nicer' children – the reason they were chosen for adoption rather than the others. As this was not accounted for it is hard to be sure that the results of the study did not simply reflect the individual differences between the children.

Although findings indicate that recovery from privation is possible under the right circumstances, Clarke and Clarke (1976) suggest that the children may not have been as well adjusted as Tizard and Hodges suggested. Instead they proposed a transactional model – as they believed that the recovery from privation depends on the interaction between the child and others (for example, later caregivers)

Enrichment

Enrichment programmes are specifically designed to reverse the effects of any possible social disadvantage by providing preschool children with a programme that will try to ensure that they enter school at the same level as their peers. Operation Headstart began in the USA in the 1960s and it was indeed found that the cognitive and social abilities of those attending the programmes was significantly better than those who had not been part of it.

Lazar and Darlington (1982) argued that such children were less likely to be delinquent, more likely to attend college, and, later, reportedly claimed fewer social and welfare benefits.

Tasks

1 Draw a time-line to explain the stages of emotional development and underneath describe what your time-line shows.

2 There are some specific case studies which will help you weigh up the argument as to whether or not deprivation has long-term effects, or whether these can be overcome. It would therefore be useful for you to look up Curtiss's study of Genie (1977) and Koluchova's study (1972) of Czech twins. Write an outline of each study, state what each one tells us about deprivation and any difficulties that might arise in using case studies as evidence.

3 There are many methodological problems with the research studies discussed within this section, and also ethical issues that arise from the type of work that was carried out. To aid your evaluation of the key thinkers and theories, identify such issues, either as part of a discussion group or as a written exercise.

Essay questions

"Critically discuss the emotional development of infants"

This requires you to focus predominantly on the evidence presented in the first half of this section and on the task involving your time-line. Initially it will help to outline what you understand the term 'emotional development' to mean before proceeding to a discussion of the various stages involved. You must be aware, however, that simply listing months and developments as has been done at the start of this section, is not sufficient. This would give you very little text. Remember, this book is a course companion and is not designed to replace your textbooks. You will therefore need to carry out extra research to identify studies that support the various stages of development outlined here. Do not forget that you will also need to go on and critically evaluate such work.

"To what extent does research (theories/studies) support the view that maternal deprivation/privation can have long-term effects on individuals?"

This is a vast topic and the key to producing a successful essay on the matter will be careful planning and selective use of the evidence. For example, the question offers a choice of deprivation or privation and you may want to consider addressing just one of these areas. This will allow you to define the concept, and outline and then evaluate the appropriate research evidence. To try and cover both may simply mean that you give a superficial outline of the appropriate studies and a list of criticisms, without engaging with the material or fully evaluating the research involved. The most critical study as evidence for the effects of deprivation is Bowlby's 44 thieves and you will need to evaluate both this study itself and the concept that deprivation has long-term effects more generally, including other research studies demonstrating this. You could make use of the case study task above or indeed other studies that Bowlby later conducted, such as his work on children who had been isolated because of TB (Bowlby et al., 1956). Similarly, privation requires some discussion of the work by Hodges and Tizard, which shows mixed evidence on the long-term effects. Again a critical look at this view is then required before drawing any conclusions about general ability to overcome deprivation/privation.

Common Pitfalls

- *Be sure that you are able to define all of the key terms and, most critically, do not mix up deprivation (loss of an attachment) with privation (never had the opportunity to form one).*
- *When outlining the stages of emotional development remember to support this with actual evidence; do not just write a chronological list.*
- *When discussing the theories of attachment, or the work of the key thinkers, ensure that your discussion is supported by the relevant key studies. It is not sufficient just to outline a theory; you must ensure that you show yourself to be a true psychologist and back up what you say with actual evidence.*
- *Remember that this section looks at the effects of deprivation and privation on emotional development and how enrichment programmes have a role to play. Always ensure you go beyond a list of studies and place them in the context of this argument as a whole.*
- *It will help if you can make sure you understand which theories/key thinkers claim that emotional development/attachment is due to nature, which claim it is nurture, and if there is any role for either.*

Textbook Guide

AINSWORTH, M. D. S. & BELL, S. M. (1970). Attachment, exploration and separation: illustrated by the behaviour of one-year-olds in a Strange Situation, *Child Development, 41,* 49–65. A key study which fully outlines the procedure involved in this study and also gives a fuller description of the classification of attachment types.

BOWLBY, J. (1944). Forty-four juvenile thieves: their characters and home lives. *International Journal of Psychoanalysis, 25,* 107–27. This covers Bowlby's classic work in detail and is a must for any developmental psychologist.

BOWLBY, J., AINSWORTH, M., BOSTON, M., AND ROSENBLUTH, D. (1956). The effects of mother–child separation: a follow-up study. *British Journal of Medical Psychology, 29,* 211–47. As an aid to writing the last essay outlined above, reading this will provide an alternative perspective on the view that all types of deprivation automatically lead to negative effects.

part three
study, writing and revision skills*

*in collaboration with David McIlroy

3.1

introduction

If you work your way carefully through this section you should at the end be better equipped to profit from your lectures, benefit from your seminars, construct your essays efficiently, develop effective revision strategies and respond comprehensively to the pressures of exam situations. In the five sections that lie ahead you will be presented with: checklists and bullet points to focus your attention on key issues; exercises to help you participate actively in the learning experience; illustrations and analogies to enable you to anchor learning principles in everyday events and experiences; worked examples to demonstrate the use of such features as structure, headings and continuity; tips that provide practical advice in nutshell form.

In the exercises that are presented each student should decide how much effort they would like to invest in each exercise, according to individual preferences and requirements. Some of the points in the exercises will be covered in the text, either before or after the exercise. You might prefer to read each section right through before going back to tackle the exercises. Suggested answers are provided in italics after some of the exercises, so avoid these if you prefer to work through the exercises on your own. The aim is to prompt you to reflect on the material, remember what you have read and trigger you to add your own thoughts. Space is provided for you to write your responses down in a few words, or you may prefer to reflect on them within your own mind. However, writing will help you to slow down and digest the material and may also enable you to process the information at a deeper level of learning.

Finally, the overall aim of the section is to point you to the keys for academic and personal development. The twin emphases of academic development and personal qualities are stressed throughout. By giving attention to these factors you will give yourself the toolkit you will need to excel in your psychology course.

3.2

how to get the most out of your lectures

What this section will give you. How to:

- make the most of your lecture notes
- prepare your mind for new terms
- develop an independent approach to learning
- write efficient summary notes from lectures
- take the initiative in building on your lectures

Keeping in context

According to higher educational commentators and advisors, best quality learning is facilitated when it is set within an overall learning context. It should be the responsibility of your tutors to provide a context for you to learn in, but it is your responsibility to see the overall context, and you can do this even before your first lecture begins. Such a panoramic view can be achieved by becoming familiar with the outline content both of psychology as a subject and of the entire study programme. Before you go into each lecture you should briefly remind yourself of where it fits into the overall scheme of things. Think, for example, of how more confident you feel when you move into a new city (for example to attend university) once you become familiar with your bearings – that is, where you live in relation to college, shops, stores, buses, trains, places of entertainment, etc.

The same principle applies to your course – find your way around your study programme and locate the position of each lecture within this overall framework.

Use of lecture notes

It is always beneficial to do some preliminary reading before you enter a lecture. If lecture notes are provided in advance (electronically, for example), then print these out, read over them and bring them with you to the lecture. You can insert question marks on issues where you will need further clarification. Some lecturers prefer to provide full notes, some prefer to make skeleton outlines available and some prefer to issue no notes at all! If notes are provided, take full advantage and supplement these with your own notes as you listen. In a later section on memory techniques you will see that humans possess the ability for 're-learning savings' – that is, it is easier to learn material the second time round, as it is evident that we have a capacity to hold residual memory deposits. So some basic preparation will equip you with a great advantage – you will be able to 'tune in' and think more clearly about the lecture than you would have done without the preliminary work.

> *If you set yourself too many tedious tasks at the early stages of your academic programme you may lose some motivation and momentum. A series of short, simple, achievable tasks can give your mind the 'lubrication' it needs. For example, you are more likely to maintain preliminary reading for a lecture if you set modest targets.*

Mastering technical terms

Let us assume that in an early lecture you are introduced to a number of new terms such as 'paradigm', 'empirical' and 'ecological validity'. If you are hearing these and other terms for the first time, you could end up with a headache! New words can be threatening, especially if you have to face a string of them in one lecture. The uncertainty about the new terms may impair your ability to benefit fully from the lecture, and therefore hinder the quality of your learning. Psychology requires technical terms and the use of them is unavoidable. However, when you have heard a term a number of times it will not seem as daunting as it initially was. It is claimed that individuals may have particular strengths in the scope of their vocabulary. Some people may have a good recognition vocabulary – they immediately know what a word means when they read it or hear it in context. Others have a good command of language when they speak – they have an ability to recall words freely. Still others are more fluent in recall when they write – words seem to flow rapidly for them when they engage in the dynamics of writing. You can work at developing all three approaches in your course, and the checklist below the next paragraph may be of some help in mastering and marshalling the terms you hear in lectures.

In terms of learning new words, it will be very useful if you can first try to work out what they mean from their context when you first encounter them. You might be much better at this than you imagine, especially if there is only one word in the sentence that you do not understand. It would also be very useful if you could obtain a small indexed notebook and use this to build up your own glossary of terms. In this way you could include a definition of a word, an example of its use, where it fits into a theory and any practical application of it.

Checklist: Mastering terms used in your lectures

✓   Read lecture notes before the lectures and list any unfamiliar terms.

✓   Read over the listed terms until you are familiar with their sound.

✓   Try to work out meanings of terms from their context.

✓   Do not suspend learning the meaning of a term indefinitely.

✓   Write out a sentence that includes the new word (do this for each word).

✓   Meet with other students and test each other with the technical terms.

✓   Jot down new words you hear in lectures and check out the meaning soon afterwards.

Your confidence will greatly increase when you begin to follow the flow of arguments that contain technical terms and, more especially, when you can freely use the terms yourself in speaking and writing.

Developing independent study

In the current educational ethos there are the twin aims of cultivating teamwork/group activities and independent learning. There is not necessarily a conflict between the two, as they should complement each other. For example, if you are committed to independent learning you have more to offer other students when you work in small groups, and you will also be prompted to follow up on the leads given by them. Furthermore, the guidelines given to you in lectures are designed to lead you into deeper independent study. The issues raised in lectures are pointers to provide direction and structure for your extended personal pursuit. Your aim should invariably be to build on what you are given, and you should never think of merely returning the bare bones of the lecture material in a coursework essay or exam.

It is always very refreshing to a marker to be given work from a student that contains recent studies that the examiner had not previously encountered.

Note-taking strategy

Note-taking in lectures is an art that you will only perfect with practice and by trial and error. Each student should find the formula that works best for him or her. What works for one, may not work for the other. Some students can write more quickly than others, some are better at shorthand than others and some are better at deciphering their own scrawl! The problem will always be to try to find a balance between concentrating beneficially on what you hear, and making sufficient notes that will enable you to comprehend later what you have heard. You should not however become frustrated by the fact that you will not understand immediately or remember everything you have heard.

By being present at a lecture, and by making some attempt to comprehend what you hear, you will already have a substantial advantage over those students who do not attend.

Checklist: Note-taking in lectures

✓ Develop the note-taking strategy that works best for you.

✓ Work at finding a balance between listening and writing.

✓ Make optimal use of shorthand (for example, a few key words may summarise a story).

✓ Too much writing may impair the flow of the lecture for you.

✓ Too much writing may impair the quality of your notes.

✓ Some limited notes are better than none.

✓ Good note-taking may facilitate deeper processing of information.

✓ It is essential to 'tidy up' notes as soon as possible after a lecture.

✓ Reading over notes soon after lectures will consolidate your learning.

Developing the lecture

Some educationalists have criticised the value of lectures because they allege that these are a mode of merely 'passive learning'. This can certainly be an accurate conclusion to arrive at (that is, if students approach lectures in the wrong way) and lecturers can work to devise ways of making a lecture more interactive. For example, they can make use of interactive handouts or by posing questions during the lecture and giving time out for students to reflect on these. Other possibilities are short discussions at given junctures in the lecture or use of small groups within the session. As a student you do not have to enter a lecture in passive mode and you can ensure that you are not merely a passive recipient of information by taking steps to develop the lecture content yourself. A list of suggestions is presented below to help you take the initiative in developing the lecture content.

Checklist: Avoid lecture being a passive experience

✓ Try to interact with the lecture material by asking questions.

✓ Highlight points that you would like to develop in personal study.

✓ Trace connections between the lecture and other parts of your study programme.

✓ Bring together notes from the lecture and other sources.

✓ Restructure the lecture outline into your own preferred format.

✓ Think of ways in which aspects of the lecture material could be applied.

✓ Design ways in which aspects of the lecture material could be illustrated.

✓ If the lecturer invites questions, make a note of all the questions asked.

✓ Follow up on issues of interest that have arisen out of the lecture.

You can contribute to this active involvement in a lecture by engaging with the material before, during and after it is delivered.

EXERCISE

You might now like to attempt to summarise (and/or add) some factors that would help you to capitalise fully on the benefits of a lecture.

....

....

....

....

....

3.3	
how to make the most of seminars	

What this section will give you. How to:

- be aware of the value of seminars
- focus on links to learning
- recognise qualities you can use repeatedly
- manage potential problems in seminars
- prepare yourself adequately for seminars

Not to be underestimated

Seminars are often optional in a degree programme and are sometimes poorly attended because they are underestimated. Some students may be convinced that the lecture is the truly authoritative way to receive quality information. Undoubtedly, lectures play an important role in an academic programme, but seminars have a unique contribution to learning that will complement lectures. Other students may feel that their time would be better spent in personal study. Again, private study is unquestionably essential for personal learning and development, but you will nevertheless diminish your learning experience if you neglect seminars. If seminars were to be removed from academic programmes, then something really important would be lost.

Checklist: Some useful features of seminars

✓ Can identify problems that you had not thought of.
✓ Can clear up confusing issues.
✓ Allows you to ask questions and make comments.
✓ Can help you develop friendships and teamwork.
✓ Enables you to refresh and consolidate your knowledge.
✓ Can help you sharpen motivation and redirect study efforts.

An asset to complement other learning activities

In higher education at the present time there is emphasis on variety – variety in delivery, learning experience, learning styles and assessment methods. The seminar is deemed to hold an important place within the overall scheme of teaching, learning and assessment. In some programmes the seminars are directly linked to the assessment task. Whether or not they have such a place in your course, they will provide you with a unique opportunity to learn and develop.

In a seminar you will hear a variety of contributions, and different perspectives and emphases. You will have the chance to interrupt and the experience of being interrupted! You will also learn that you can get things wrong and still survive! It is often the case that when one student admits that they did not know some important piece of information, other students quickly follow on to the same admission in the wake of this. If you can learn to ask questions and not feel stupid, then seminars will be an asset for learning and a life-long educational quality.

Creating the right climate in seminars

It has been said that we have been given only one mouth to talk, but two ears to listen. One potential problem with seminars is that some students may take a while to learn this lesson, and other students may have to help hasten them on the way (graciously but firmly!). In lectures your main role is to listen and take notes, but in seminars there is the challenge to strike the balance between listening and speaking. It is important to make a beginning in speaking even if it is just to repeat something that you agree with. You can also learn to disagree in an agreeable way. For example, you can raise a question against what someone else has said and pose this in a good tone – for example, 'If that is the case, does that not mean that ...?' In addition, it is perfectly possible to disagree with others by avoiding personal attacks such as, 'That was a really stupid thing to say', or 'I thought you knew better than that', or 'I'm surprised that you don't know that by now.' Educationalists say that it is important to have the right climate to learn in, and the avoidance of unnecessary conflict will foster such a climate.

EXERCISE

Suggest what can be done to reach agreement (set ground rules) that would help keep seminars running smoothly and harmoniously.

....

....

....

....

....

Some suggestions are: Appoint someone to guide and control the discussion, invite individuals to prepare in advance to make a contribution, hand out agreed discussion questions at some point prior to the seminar, stress at the beginning that no one should monopolise the discussion and emphasise that there must be no personal attacks on any individual (state clearly what this means). Also you could invite and encourage quieter students to participate and assure each person that their contribution is valued.

Links in learning and transferable skills

An important principle in learning to progress from shallow to deep learning is developing the capacity to make connecting links between themes or topics and across subjects. This also applies to the various learning activities such as lectures, seminars, fieldwork, computer searches and private study. Another factor to think about is, 'What skills can I develop, or improve on, from seminars that I can use across my study programme?' A couple of examples of key skills are the ability to communicate and the capacity to work within a team. These are skills that you will be able to use at various points in your course (transferable), but you are not likely to develop them within the formal setting of a lecture.

EXERCISE

Write out or think about (a) three things that give seminars value, and (b) three useful skills that you can develop in seminars.

(a)

....

....

....

(b)

....

....

....

In the above exercises, for (a) you could have: variety of contributors, flexibility to spend more time on problematic issues and an agreed agenda settled at the beginning of the seminar. For (b) you could have: communication, conflict resolution and teamwork.

> *A key question that you should bring to every seminar: 'How does this seminar connect with my other learning activities and my assessments?'*

An opportunity to contribute

If you have never made a contribution to a seminar before, you may need something to use as an 'ice-breaker'. It does not matter if your first contribution is only a sentence or two – the important thing is to make a start. One way to do this is to make brief notes as others contribute, and while you are doing this, a question or two might arise in your mind. If your first contribution is a question, that is a good start. Or it may be that you will be able to point out some connection between what others have said, or identify conflicting opinions that need to be resolved. If you have already begun making contributions, it is important that you keep the momentum going, and do not allow yourself to lapse back into the safe cocoon of shyness.

EXERCISE

See if you can suggest how you might resolve some of the following problems that might hinder you from making a contribution to seminars.

- **One student who dominates and monopolises the discussion.**

- **Someone else has already said what you really want to say.**

- **Fear that someone else will correct you and make you feel stupid.**

- **Feel that your contribution might be seen as short and shallow.**

- **A previous negative experience puts you off making any more contributions.**

Strategies for benefiting from your seminar experience

If you are required to bring a presentation to your seminar, you might want to consult a full chapter on presentations in a complementary study guide (McIlroy, 2003). Alternatively, you may be content with the summary points presented after the checklist. In order to benefit from discussions in seminars (the focus of this section), some useful summary nutshells are now presented as a checklist.

Checklist: How to benefit from seminars

✓   Do some preparatory reading.
✓   Familiarise yourself with the main ideas to be addressed.
✓   Make notes during the seminar.

✓ Make some verbal contribution, even a question.

✓ Remind yourself of the skills you can develop.

✓ Trace learning links from the seminar to other subjects/topics on your programme.

✓ Make brief bullet points on what you should follow up on.

✓ Read over your notes as soon as possible after the seminar.

✓ Continue discussion with fellow students after the seminar has ended.

If required to give a presentation:

✓ Have a practice run with friends.

✓ If using visuals, do not obstruct them.

✓ Check out beforehand that all equipment works.

✓ Space out points clearly on visuals (large and legible).

✓ Time talk by visuals (e.g. 5 slides by 15-minute talk = 3 minutes per slide).

✓ Make sure your talk synchronises with the slide on view at any given point.

✓ Project your voice so that all in the room can hear.

✓ Inflect your voice and do not stand motionless.

✓ Spread eye contact around audience.

✓ Avoid twin extremes of fixed gaze at individuals and never looking at anyone.

✓ Better to fall a little short of time allocation as run over it.

✓ Be selective in what you choose to present.

✓ Map out where you are going and summarise main points at the end.

3.4	
essay-writing tips	

What this section will give you. How to:

- quickly engage with the main arguments
- channel your passions constructively
- note your main arguments in an outline

- find and focus on your central topic questions
- weave quotations into your essay

Getting into the flow

In essay writing one of your first aims should be to get your mind active and engaged with your subject. Tennis players like to go out onto the court and hit the ball back and forth just before the competitive match begins. This allows them to judge the bounce of the ball, feel its weight against their racket, get used to the height of the net, the parameters of the court and other factors such as temperature, light, sun and the crowd. In the same way you can 'warm up' for your essay by tossing the ideas to and fro within your head before you begin to write. This will allow you to think within the framework of your topic, and this will be especially important if you are coming to the subject for the first time.

The tributary principle

A tributary is a stream that runs into a main river as it wends its way to the sea. Similarly, in an essay you should ensure that every idea you introduce is moving toward the overall theme you are addressing. Your idea might of course be relevant to a subheading that is in turn relevant to a main heading. Every idea you introduce is to be a 'feeder' into the flowing theme. In addition to tributaries, there can also be 'distributaries', which are streams that flow away from the river. In an essay these would represent the ideas that run away from the main stream of thought and leave the reader trying to work out what their relevance may have been. It is one thing to have grasped your subject thoroughly, but quite another to convince your reader that this is the case. Your aim should be to build up ideas sentence by sentence and paragraph by paragraph, until you have communicated your clear purpose to the reader.

It is important in essay writing that you not only include material that is relevant, but that you also make the linking statements that show the connection to the reader.

Listing and linking the key concepts

Psychology has central concepts that can sometimes be usefully labelled by a single word. Course textbooks may include a glossary of terms and these provide a direct route to beginning an efficient mastery of the topic. The central words or terms are the essential raw materials that you will need to build upon. Ensure that you learn the words and their definitions, and that you can go on to link the key words together so that in your learning activities you will add understanding to your basic memory work.

It is useful to list your key words under general headings if that is possible and logical. You may not always see the connections immediately but when you later come back to a problem that seemed intractable, you will often find that your thinking is much clearer.

Example: Write an essay on 'gender development'.

You might decide to draft your outline points in the following manner (or you might prefer to use a mind-map approach):

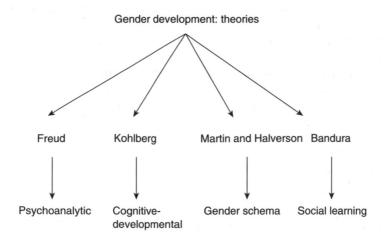

An adversarial system

In higher education students are required to make the transition from descriptive to critical writing. If you can, think of the critical approach as like a law case that is being conducted where there is both a prosecution and a defence. Your concern should be for objectivity, transparency and fairness. No matter how passionately you may feel about a given cause you must not allow information to be filtered out because of your personal prejudice. An essay is not to become a crusade for a cause in which the contrary arguments are not addressed in an even-handed manner. This means that you should show awareness that opposite views are held and you should at least represent these as accurately as possible.

> *Your role as the writer is like that of the judge in that you must ensure that all the evidence is heard, and that nothing will compromise either party.*

Stirring up passions

The above points do not of course mean that you are not entitled to a personal persuasion or to feel passionately about your subject. On the contrary, such feelings may well be a marked advantage if you can bring them under control and channel them into balanced, effective writing (see example below). Some students may be struggling at the other end of the spectrum – being required to write on a topic that they feel quite indifferent about. As you engage with your topic and toss the ideas around in your mind, you will hopefully find that your interest is stimulated, if only at an intellectual level initially. How strongly you feel about a topic, or how much you are interested in it, may depend on whether you choose the topic yourself or whether it has been given to you as an obligatory assignment.

> *It is important that in a large project (such as a dissertation) you choose a topic for which you can maintain your motivation, momentum and enthusiasm.*

Example: An issue that may stir up passions.

Arguments for and against the view that privation has long-term effects:

For:

- Privated children show more attention-seeking behaviour, restlessness, disobedience and poor peer relationships at age 8 (Hodges & Tizard, 1989).
- At age 16 they were rated less favourably than their siblings, were less affectionate, identified less with their parents and did not want to be involved in discussions.

Against:

- Privation has no effect, as Hodges and Tizard found that both groups showed similar relationships to adults and peers outside of the family, seeking more adult attention and approval, were more likely to have difficulties with their peer group and less likely to have a special friend or use peers for emotional support.
- Not all children could be traced so the study gives an unrepresentative view on the effects of privation.
- A child's individual characteristics have not been accounted for sufficiently when looking at the outcomes for privated children.

Structuring an outline

Whenever you sense a flow of inspiration to write on a given subject, it is essential that you put this into a structure that will allow your inspiration to be communicated clearly. It is a basic principle in all walks of life that structure and order facilitate good communication. Therefore, when you have the flow of inspiration in your essay you must get this into a structure that will allow the marker to recognise the true quality of your work. For example, you might plan for an Introduction, Conclusion, three main headings – each of these with several subheadings (see example below). Moreover, you may decide not to include your headings in your final presentation – that is, just use them initially to structure and balance your arguments. Once you have drafted this outline you can then easily sketch an Introduction, and you will have been well prepared for the Conclusion when you arrive at that point.

A good structure will help you to balance the weight of your arguments against each other, and arrange your points in the order that will facilitate the fluent progression of your argument.

Example: Write an essay that compares and contrasts theories of the developing self.

1   Similarities between theories

   (a) Agreement that there are different types of self.
   (b) Consideration of stages in achieving sense of self.

2   Differences between theories

   (a) Focus on cognitions.
   (b) Focus on nature versus nurture in formation of the self.

Finding major questions

When you are constructing a draft outline for an essay or project, you should ask what is the major question or questions you wish to address. It would be useful to make a list of all the issues that spring to mind that you might wish to tackle. The ability to design a good question is a skill that should be cultivated, and such questions will allow you to impress your assessor with the quality of your thinking.

> If you construct your ideas around key questions, this will help you focus your mind and engage effectively with your subject. Your role will be like that of a detective – exploring the evidence and investigating the findings.

Rest your case

It should be your aim to give the clear impression that your arguments are not based entirely on hunches, bias, feelings or intuition. In exams and essay questions it is usually assumed (even if not directly specified) that you will appeal to evidence to support your claims. Therefore, when you write your essay you should ensure that it is liberally sprinkled with research evidence. By the time the assessor reaches the end of your work, he or she should be convinced that your conclusions are evidence-based. A fatal flaw to be avoided is to make claims for which you have provided no authoritative source.

> *Give the clear impression that what you have asserted is derived from recognised sources (including up-to-date ones). It also looks impressive if you spread your citations across your essay rather than compressing them into a paragraph or two at the beginning and end.*

Examples: How to introduce your evidence and sources.

According to O'Neil (1999) ...
Wilson (2003) has concluded that ...
Taylor (2004) found that ...
It has been claimed by McKibben (2002) that ...
Appleby (2001) asserted that ...
A review of the evidence by Lawlor (2004) suggests that ...
Findings from a meta-analysis presented by Rea (2003) would indicate that ...

It is sensible to vary the expression used so that you are not monotonous and repetitive, and it also aids variety to introduce researchers' names at various places in the sentence (not always at the beginning). It is advisable to choose the expression that is most appropriate – for example you can make a stronger statement about reviews that have identified recurrent and predominant trends in findings as opposed to one study that appears to run contrary to all the rest.

> *Credit is given for the use of caution and discretion when this is clearly needed.*

Careful use of quotations

Although it is desirable to present a good range of cited sources, it is not judicious to present these as a 'patchwork quilt' – that is, you just paste together what others have said with little thought for interpretative comment or coherent structure. It is a good general point to aim to avoid lengthy quotes – short ones can be very effective. Aim at blending the quotations as naturally as possible into the flow of your sentences. Also, it is good to vary your practices – sometimes use short, direct, brief quotes (cite page number as well as author and year), and at times you can summarise the gist of a quote in your own words. In this case you should cite the author's name and year of publication but leave out quotation marks and page number.

> *Use your quotes and evidence in a manner that demonstrates that you have thought the issues through, and have integrated them in a manner that shows you have been focused and selective in the use of your sources.*

In terms of referencing, practice may vary from one discipline to the next, but some general points that will go a long way in contributing to good practice are:

- If a reference is cited in the text, it must be in the list at the end (and vice versa).
- Names and dates in text should correspond exactly with the list in References or Bibliography.
- List of References and Bibliography should be in alphabetical order by the surname (not the initials) of the author or first author.
- Any reference you make in the text should be traceable by the reader (they should clearly be able to identify and trace the source).

A clearly defined Introduction

In an Introduction to an essay you have the opportunity to define the problem or issue that is being addressed and to set it in context. Resist the temptation to elaborate on any issue at the introductory stage. For example, think of a music composer who throws out hints and suggestions of the motifs that the orchestra will later develop. What he or she does in the Introduction is to provide little tasters of what will follow in order to whet the audience's appetite. If you go back to the analogy of the game of tennis, you can think of the Introduction as marking out the boundaries of the court in which the game is to be played.

> *If you leave the introduction and definition of your problem until the end of your writing, you will be better placed to map out the directions that will be taken.*

An example for practice, if you wish, can be undertaken if you look back at the draft outline on writing an essay on arguments for and against the view that privation has long-term effects. Try to design an introduction for that essay in about three or four sentences.

....

....

....

....

Conclusion – adding the finishing touches

In the conclusion you should aim to tie your essay together in a clear and coherent manner. It is your last chance to leave an overall impression in your reader's mind. Therefore, you will at this stage want to do justice to your efforts and not sell yourself short. This is your opportunity to identify where the strongest evidence points or where the balance of probability lies. The conclusion to an exam question often has to be written hurriedly under the pressure of time, but with an essay (coursework) you have time to reflect on, refine and adjust the content to your satisfaction. It should be your goal to make the conclusion a smooth finish that does justice to the range of content in summary and succinct form. Do not underestimate the value of an effective conclusion. 'Sign off' your essay in a manner that brings closure to the treatment of your subject.

The conclusion enables you to demonstrate where the findings have brought us to date, to highlight the issues that remain unresolved and to point to where future research should take us.

Top-down and bottom-up clarity

An word processor gives you the opportunity to refine each sentence and paragraph in your essay. Each sentence is like a tributary that leads into the stream of the paragraph that in turn leads into the mainstream of the essay. From a 'top-down' perspective (that is, starting at the top with your major outline points), clarity is facilitated by the structure you draft in your outline. You can ensure that the subheadings are appropriately placed under the most relevant main heading, and that both sub- and main headings are arranged in logical sequence. From a 'bottom-up' perspective (that is, building up the details that 'flesh out' your main points), you should check that each sentence is a 'feeder' for the predominant concept in a given paragraph. When all this is done you can check that the transition from one point to the next is smooth rather than abrupt.

Checklist: Summary for essay writing

✓ Before you start, have a 'warm-up' by tossing the issues around in your head.

✓ List the major concepts and link them in fluent form.

✓ Design a structure (outline) that will facilitate balance, progression, fluency and clarity.

✓ Pose questions and address these in critical fashion.

✓ Demonstrate that your arguments rest on evidence and spread cited sources across your essay.

✓ Provide an Introduction that sets the scene and a Conclusion that rounds off the arguments.

EXERCISE

Attempt to write (or at least think about) some additional features that would help facilitate good essay writing.

....

....

....

....

....

In the above checklist your could have features such as originality, clarity in sentence and paragraph structure, applied aspects, addressing a subject you feel passionately about and the ability to avoid going off at a tangent.

3.5	
revision hints and tips	

What this section will give you. How to:

- map out your accumulated material for revision
- choose summary tags to guide your revision
- keep well-organised folders for revision
- make use of effective memory techniques
- revise in a way that combines bullet points and in-depth reading
- profit from the benefits of revising with others

The return journey

On a return journey you will usually pass by all the same places you had already passed when you were outward bound. If you had observed the various landmarks on your outward journey you would be likely to remember them on your return. Similarly, revision is a means to 'revisit' what you have encountered before. Familiarity with your material can help reduce anxiety, inspire confidence and fuel motivation for further learning and good performance.

> *If you are to capitalise on your revision period, then you must have your materials arranged and at hand for the time when you are ready to make your 'return journey' through your notes.*

Start at the beginning

Strategy for revision should be on your mind from your first lecture at the beginning of your academic semester. You should be like the squirrel that stores up nuts for the winter. Do not waste any lecture, tutorial, seminar, group discussion, etc., by letting the material evaporate into thin air. Get into the habit of making a few guidelines for revision after each learning activity. Keep a folder, or file, or little notebook that is reserved for revision and write out the major points that you have learned. By establishing this regular practice you will find that what you have learned becomes consolidated in your mind, and you will also be in a better position to 'import' and 'export' your material both within and across subjects.

If you do this regularly, and do not make the task too tedious, you will be amazed at how much useful summary material you have accumulated when revision time comes.

Compile summary notes

It would useful and convenient to have a little notebook or cards on which you can write outline summaries that provide you with an overview of your subject at a glance. You could also use treasury tags to hold different batches of cards together while still allowing for inserts and re-sorting. Such practical resources can easily be slipped into your pocket or bag and produced when you are on the bus or train or while sitting in a traffic jam. They would also be useful if you are standing in a queue or waiting for someone who is not in a rush! A glance over your notes will consolidate your learning and will also activate your mind to think further about your subject. Therefore it would also be useful to make a note of the questions that you would like to think about in greater depth. Your primary task is to get into the habit of constructing outline notes that will be useful for revision, and a worked example is provided below.

There is a part of the mind that will continue to work on problems when you have moved on to focus on other issues. Therefore, if you feed on useful, targeted information, your mind will continue to work on 'automatic pilot' after you have 'switched off'.

Example: Part of a course on developmental psychology would be cognitive development and your outline revision structure for this might be as follows.

1   *Key thinkers/theories*

- Piaget (1967)

- Bruner et al. (1966)

- Vygotsky (1962)

2 Evaluation of these theories

- Some believe that linguistic explanations for cognitive development can be offered rather than failure of development being due to a lack of logical competence.
- It has also been argued that pre-operational children fail on concrete operational tasks, not because of knowledge but because the researcher gives misleading cues.
- With regards to experimental validity, Piagetian tasks are abstract and artificial and therefore failure could be due to their unfamiliarity to the child. Moreover, everyday life and research have shown that cognitive competence is displayed if the tasks are recognisable ones.

Keep organised records

People who have a fulfilled career have usually developed the twin skills of time- and task-management. It is worth pausing to remember that you can use your academic training to prepare for your future career in this respect. Therefore, ensure that you do not fall short of your potential because these qualities have not been cultivated. One important tactic is to keep a folder for each subject and divide this topic by topic. You can keep your topics in the same order in which they are presented in your course lectures. Bind them together in a ring binder or folder and use subject dividers to keep them apart. Make a numbered list of the contents at the beginning of the folder, and list each topic clearly as it marks a new section in your folder. Another important practice is to place all your notes on a given topic within the appropriate section – don't put off this simple task but do it straightaway. Notes may come from lectures, seminars, tutorials, Internet searches, personal notes, etc. It is also essential that when you remove these for consultation you return them to their 'home' immediately after use.

> Academic success has as much to do with good organisation and planning, as it has to do with ability. The value of the quality material you have accumulated on your academic programme may be diminished because you have not organised it into an easily retrievable form.

Fun example: An organised record of a history of romantic relationships.

- Physical features my girl friends/boy friends have shared or differed from.
- Common and diverse personality characteristics.
- Shared and contrasting interests.
- Frequency of dates with each.

- Places frequented together.
- Contact with both circles of friends.
- Use of humour in our communication.
- Frequency and resolution of conflicts.
- Mutual generosity.
- Courtesy and consideration.
- Punctuality.
- Dress and appearance.

Let's imagine that you've had five girl friends/boy friends over the last few years. Each of the five names could be included under all of the above subjects. You could then compare them with each other – looking at what they had in common and how they differed. Moreover, you could think of the ones you liked best and least, and then look through your dossier to establish why this might have been. You could also judge who had most and least in common with you and whether you are more attracted to those who differed most from you. The questions open to you can go on and on. The real point here is that you will have gathered a wide variety of material that is organised in such a way that will allow you to use a range of evidence to come up with some satisfactory and authoritative conclusions – if that is possible in matters so directly related to the heart!

Use past papers

Revision will be very limited if it is confined to memory work. You should by all means read over your revision cards or notebook and keep the picture of the major facts in front of your mind's eye. It is also, however, essential that you become familiar with previous exam papers so that you will have some idea of how the questions are likely to be framed. Therefore, build up a good range of past exam papers (especially recent ones) and add these to your folder. When cows and sheep have grazed, they lie down and 'chew the cud'. That is, they regurgitate what they have eaten and take time to digest the food thoroughly.

> *If you think over previous exam questions, this will help you not only to recall what you have deposited in your memory, but also to develop your understanding of the issues. The questions from past exam papers, and further questions that you have developed yourself, will allow you to 'chew the cud'.*

Worked example: Evaluate theories of language development.

Immediately you can see that you will require two lists and you can begin to work on documenting your reasons under each as below:

Support: Say how each theory of language development can be supported

- Skinner (1957) saw language merely as a product of trial and error, reinforcement and behaviour shaping, which can be readily tested as a behavioural theory and is observable in the real world.
- Chomsky ([1959]86) believed that language acquisition was innate and is supported by the fact that children automatically learn it because they have an inbuilt mechanism that allows them to interpret/de-code the language they hear and its rules.
- Bruner's (1983) theory that the form of language is related to the social world and the routines that take place within it is supported by the idea that society does help provide a context for the meaning of words.
- Bruner (1983) alternatively proposed that children have a LASS (language acquisition support system) whereby language derives from the interaction between parent and child, most notably by giving language the necessary social context.

Criticisms: To evaluate, say how each theory can be criticised

- Skinner's theory cannot account for the universal stages that children seem to go through in language development, nor does it account for the similar errors made by children, for example, 'mouses' rather than 'mice' – language must therefore involve more than simply reinforcement.
- It would also be difficult to accept that the vast language produced by children, and the creativity of such language is a result of only trial and error.
- Chomsky's theory ignores the active role parents play in language development, or any possible role in learning.
- Interactionists criticise the idea that language is purely innate and propose that at least some social interaction/stimulation is required to acquire the meaning of words within the correct context.

You will have noticed that the word 'evaluate' is in the question – so your mind must go to work on making judgements. You may decide to work through problems first and then through pleasures, or it may be your preference to compare point with point as you go along. Whatever conclusion you come to may be down to personal subjective preference but at least you will have worked through all the issues from both standpoints. The lesson is to ensure that part of your revision should include critical thinking as well as memory work.

You cannot think adequately without the raw materials provided by your memory deposits.

Employ effective mnemonics (memory aids)

'Mnemonics' can be simply defined as aids to memory – devices that will help you recall information that might otherwise be difficult to retrieve from memory. For example, if you find an old toy in the attic of your house, it may suddenly trigger a flood of childhood memories associated with it. Mnemonics can therefore be thoughts of as keys that open memory's storehouse.

Visualisation is one technique that can be used to aid memory. For example, the Location Method is where a familiar journey is visualised and you 'place' the facts that you wish to remember at various landmarks along the journey – such as a bus stop, a car park, a shop, a store, a bend, a police station, a traffic light, etc. This has the advantage of making an association between the information you have to learn and other material that is already firmly embedded and structured in your memory. Therefore, once the relevant memory is activated, a dynamic 'domino effect' will be triggered. However, there is no reason why you cannot use a whole toolkit of mnemonics. Some examples and illustrations of these are presented below.

> *If you can arrange your subject matter in a logical sequence this will ensure that your series of facts will also connect with each other and one will trigger the other in recall.*
> *You can use memory devices either at the stage of initial learning or when you later return to consolidate.*

Example: Location method – defined above.

Visualisation

Turn information into pictures – e.g. the example given about the problems and pleasures of pets could be envisaged as two tug-of-war teams that pull against each other. You could visualise each player as an argument and have the label written on his or her T-shirt. The war could start with two players and then be joined by another two and so on. In addition you could compare each player's weight to the strength of each argument. You might also want to make use of colour – your favourite colour for the winning team and the colour you dislike most for the losers!

Alliteration's artful aid

Find a series of words that all begin with the same sounds. See the example below related to the experiments of Ebbinghaus.

Peg system

'Hang' information onto a term so that when you hear the term you will remember the ideas connected with it (an umbrella term). For example in aggression there are different kinds – biological, chronological, socio-logical and psychological. Under biological you could remember psychodynamic and ethological.

Hierarchical system

This is a development of the previous point, with higher-order, middle-order and lower-order terms. For example, you could think of the continents of the world (higher order), and then group these into the countries under them (middle order). Under countries you could have cities, rivers and mountains (lower order).

Acronyms

Take the first letter of all the key words and make a word from these.

Mind-maps

These have become very popular – they allow you to draw lines that stretch out from the central idea, and to develop the subsidiary ideas in the same way. It is a little like the pegging and hierarchical methods combined and turned sideways! The method has the advantage of giving you the complete picture at a glance, although mind-maps can become complex works of art!

Rhymes and chimes

Words that rhyme and words that end with a similar sound (such as com-memoration, celebration, anticipation). These provide another dimension to memory work by including sound. Memory can be enhanced when information is processed in various modalities – hearing, seeing, speaking, visualising.

A confidence booster

At the end of the nineteenth century, Hermann Ebbinghaus and his assistant memorised lists of nonsense words (that is, words that could not be remembered by being attached to meaning), and then endeavoured to recall these. What they discovered was:

- Some words could be recalled freely from memory, while others appeared to be forgotten.
- Words that could not be recalled were later recognised as belonging to the lists (that is, were not new additions).

- When the lists were jumbled into a different sequence, the experimenters were able to re-order them into the original sequence.
- When the words that were 'forgotten' were learned again, the learning process was much easier the second time (that is, there was evidence of re-learning savings).

The four points of this experiment can be remembered by alliteration: Recall, Recognition, Reconstruction and Re-learning savings. This experiment has been described as a confidence booster because it demonstrates that memory is more powerful than is often imagined, especially when we consider that Ebbinghaus and his assistant did not have the advantage of processing the meaning of the words.

Alternate between methods

It is not sufficient to present outline points in response to an exam question (although it is better to do this than nothing if you have run out of time in your exam). Your aim should be to put 'meat on the bones' by adding substance, evidence and arguments to your basic points. You should work at finding the balance between the two methods – outline revision cards might be best reserved for short bus journeys, whereas extended reading might be better fitted into for longer revision slots at home or in the library. Your ultimate goal should be to bring together an effective, working approach that will enable you to face your exam questions comprehensively and confidently.

> In revision it is useful to alternate between scanning over your outline points, and reading through your notes, articles, chapters, etc. in an in-depth manner. Also, the use of different times, places and methods will provide you with the variety that might prevent monotony and facilitate freshness.

Worked example: Imagine that you are doing a course on developmental psychology.

Your major outline topics might be:

- Research methods in developmental psychology
- Perceptual development
- Cognitive development

- Language development
- Physical/motor development
- Influences of biology/heredity on behaviour
- Social influences on behaviour
- Development of self and identity
- Gender development
- Emotional development, deprivation and enrichment

This outline would be your overall, bird's-eye view of the course. You could then choose one of the topics and have all your key terms under that. For example, under gender development you might have listed psychoanalytic theory, cognitive-developmental theory, gender schema theory, social learning theory, biosocial theory and sociobiological theory.

If you alternate between memory work and reading, you will soon be able to think through the processes by just looking at your outlines.

Revising with others

If you can find a few other students to revise with, this will provide another fresh approach to the last stages of your learning. First ensure that others carry their share of the workload and are not merely using the hard work of others as a short-cut to success. Of course you should think of group sessions as one of the strings on your violin, but not the only string. This collective approach will allow you to assess your strengths and weaknesses (showing you where you are off track), and to benefit from the resources and insights of others. Before you meet up you can each design some questions for the whole group to address. The group could also go through past exam papers and discuss the points that might provide an effective response to each question. It should not be the aim of the group to provide standard and identical answers for each group member to mimic. Group work is currently deemed to be advantageous by educationalists, and teamwork is held to be a desirable employability quality.

Each individual should aim to use their own style and content while drawing on and benefiting from the group's resources.

Make a list of the advantages and disadvantages of revising in small groups.

Advantages   **Disadvantages**

1. ....

2. ....

3. ....

4. ....

5. ....

Can the disadvantages be eliminated or at least minimised?

Checklist: Good study habits for revision time.

✓ Set a date for the 'official' beginning of revision and prepare for 'revision mode'.

✓ Do not force cramming by leaving revision too late.

✓ Take breaks from revision to avoid saturation.

✓ Indulge in relaxing activities to give your mind a break from pressure.

✓ Minimise or eliminate use of alcohol during the revision season.

✓ Get into a good rhythm of sleep to allow your mind to be refreshed.

✓ Avoid excessive caffeine, especially at night so that sleep is not disrupted.

✓ Try to adhere to regular eating patterns.

✓ Try to have a brisk walk in fresh air each day (for example, in the park).

✓ Avoid excessive dependence on junk food and snacks.

EXERCISE

Write your own checklist on what to add to the revision process to ensure it is not just a memory exercise.

....

....

....

....

....

In the above exercise, what you could add to memory work during revision might include using past exam papers, setting problem-solving tasks, doing drawings to show connections and directions between various concepts, explaining concepts to student friends in joint revision sessions and devising your own mock exam questions.

3.6	
exam tips	

What this section will give you. How to:

- develop strategies for controlling your nervous energy
- tackle worked examples of time- and task-management in exams
- attend to the practical details associated with the exam
- stay focused on the exam questions
- link revision outlines to strategy for addressing exam questions
- attend to the practical exam details that will help keep panic at bay
- use strategies that keep you task-focused during the exam
- select and apply relevant points from your prepared outlines

Handling your nerves

Exam nerves are not unusual and it has been concluded that test anxiety arises because of the perception that your performance is being evaluated, that the consequences are likely to be serious and that you are working under the pressure of a time restriction. However, it has also been asserted that the activation of the autonomic nervous system is adaptive in that is designed to prompt us to take action in order to avoid danger. If you focus on the task at hand rather than on feeding a downward negative spiral in your thinking patterns, this will help you keep your nerves under control. In the run-up to your exams you can practise some simple relaxation techniques that will help you bring stress under control.

It is a very good thing if you can interpret your nervous reactions positively, but the symptoms are more likely to be problematic if you interpret them negatively, pay too much attention to them or allow them to interfere with your exam preparation or performance.

Practices that may help reduce or buffer the effects of exam stress:

- listening to music
- going for a brisk walk
- simple breathing exercises
- some muscle relaxation
- watching a movie
- enjoying some laughter
- doing some exercise
- relaxing in a bath (with music if preferred)

The best choice is going to be the one (or combination) that works best for you – perhaps to be discovered by trial and error. Some of the above techniques can be practised on the morning of the exam, and even the memory of them can be used just before the exam. For example you could run over a relaxing tune in your head, and have this echo inside you as you enter the exam room. The idea behind all this is, first, that stress levels must come down, and second, that relaxing thoughts will serve to displace stressful reactions. It has been said that stress is the body's call to take action, but anxiety is a maladaptive response to that call.

It is important you are convinced that your stress levels can come under control, and that you can have a say in this. Do not give anxiety a vacuum to work in.

Time management with examples

The all-important matter as you approach an exam is to develop the belief that you can take control of the situation. As you work through the list of issues that you need to address, you will be able to tick them off one by one. One of the issues you will need to be clear about before the exam is the length of time you should allocate to each question. Sometimes this can be quite simple (although it is always necessary to read the rubric carefully) – for example, if two questions are to be answered in a two-hour paper, you should allow one hour for each question. If it is a two-hour paper with one essay question and 5 shorter answers, you could allow one hour for the essay and 12 minutes each for the shorter questions. However, you always need to check out the weighting for the marks on each question, and remember also to deduct whatever time it takes you to read over the paper and to choose your questions. See if you can work out a time-management strategy in each of the following scenarios. More importantly, give yourself some practice on the papers you are likely to face.

> Remember to check if the structure of your exam paper is the same as in previous years, and do not forget that excessive time on your 'strongest' question may not compensate for very poor answers to other questions Also ensure that you read the rubric carefully in the exam.

EXERCISE

Examples for working out the division of exam labour by time

1. A 3-hour paper with 4 compulsory questions (equally weighted in marks).

2. A 3-hour paper with 2 essays and 10 short questions (each of the three sections carries one third of the marks).

3. A 2-hour paper with 2 essay questions and 100 multiple-choice questions (half marks are on the two essays and half marks on the multiple-choice section).

Get into the calculating frame of mind and be sure to have the calculations done before the exam. Ensure that the structure of the exam has not changed since the last one. Also deduct the time taken to read over the paper in allocating time to each question.

Suggested answers to previous exercise.

1 *This allows 45 minutes for each question (4 questions × 45 minutes = 2 hours). However, if you allow 40 minutes for each question this will give you 20 minutes (4 questions × 5 minutes) to read over the paper and plan your outlines.*

2 *In this example you can spend 1 hour on each of the two major questions, and 1 hour on the 10 short questions. For the two major questions you could allow 10 minutes for reading and planning on each, and 50 minutes for writing. In the 10 short questions, you could allow 6 minutes in total for each (10 questions × 6 minutes = 60 minutes). However, if you allow approximately 1 minute reading and planning time, this will allow 5 minutes' writing time for each question.*

3 *In this case you have to divide 120 minutes by 2 questions – this allows 40 minutes for each. You could for example allow 5 minutes reading/planning time for each essay and 35 minutes for writing (or 10 minutes reading/planning and 30 minutes writing). After you have completed the two questions you are left with 40 minutes to tackle the 100 multiple-choice questions.*

You may not be able to achieve total precision in planning time for tasks, but you will have a greater feeling of control and confidence if you have some reference points to guide you.

Task management with examples

After you have decided on the questions you wish to address, you then need to plan your answers. Some students prefer to plan all outlines and draft work at the beginning, while others prefer to plan and address one answer before proceeding to address the next question. Decide on your strategy before you enter the exam room and stick to your plan. When you have done your draft outline as rough work, you should allocate an appropriate time for each section. This will prevent you from excessive treatment of some aspects while falling short on other parts. Such careful planning will help you achieve balance, fluency and symmetry.

> *Be aware of time limitations and this will help you to write succinctly, keep focused on the task and do not dress up your responses with unnecessary padding.*

Some students put as much effort into their rough work as they do into their exam essay.

> *An over-elaborate mind-map may give the impression that the essay is little more than a repetition of this detailed structure, and that the quality of the content has suffered because too much time was spent on the plan.*

EXERCISE

Work out the time allocation for the following outline, allowing for one hour on the question. Deduct 10 minutes taken at the beginning for choice and planning.

Discuss theories of attachment

1. Ethology

(a) **is an evolutionary and instinctive process.**
(b) **supported by Lorenz's ideas on imprinting.**
(c) **Criticisms of theory.**

2. Bowlby's theory

(a) **Attachment is due to an innate need to form a monotrophic bond.**
(b) **Support for model – Bowlby's 44 thieves study.**
(c) **Criticisms of theory.**

3. Learning theory

(a) **Attachment is learnt as it brings satisfaction and comfort.**
(b) **can be supported by Schaffer's research indicating multiple attachment formation.**
(c) **Criticisms of theory.**

Attend to practical details

This short section is designed to remind you of the practical details that should be attended to in preparation for an exam. There are always students who turn up late, or to the wrong venue or for the wrong exam, or do not turn up at all! Check and re-check that you have all the details of each exam correctly noted. What you don't need is to arrive late and then have to tame your panic reactions. The exam season is the time when you should aim to be at your best.

> *Turn up to the right venue in good time so that you can quieten your mind and bring your stress under control.*

Make note of the following details and check that you have taken control of each one.

Checklist: Practical exam details

✓ Check that you have the correct venue.
✓ Make sure you know how to locate the venue before the exam day.
✓ Ensure that the exam time you have noted is accurate.
✓ Allow sufficient time for your journey and consider the possibility of delays.
✓ Bring an adequate supply of stationery and include back-up.
✓ Bring a watch for your time and task management.
✓ You may need some liquid such as a small bottle of still water.
✓ You may also need to bring some tissues.
✓ Observe whatever exam regulations your university/college has set in place.
✓ Fill in required personal details before the exam begins.

Control wandering thoughts

In a simple study conducted in the 1960s Ganzer (1968) found that students who frequently lifted their heads and looked away from their scripts during exams tended to perform poorly. This makes sense because it implies that the students were taking too much time out when they should have been on task. *One way to fail your exam is to get* up and walk out of the test room, but another way is to 'leave' the test room mentally by being preoccupied with distracting thoughts. The distracting thoughts may be either related to the exam itself or totally irrelevant to it. The net effect of both these forms of intrusion is to distract you from the task at hand and impair your test performance. Read over the two lists of distracting thoughts presented below.

Typical test-relevant thoughts (evaluative)

- I wish I had prepared better.
- What will the examiner think?
- Others are doing better than me.
- What I am writing is nonsense.
- Can't remember important details.

Characteristic test-irrelevant thoughts (non-evaluative)

- Looking forward to this weekend.
- Which video should I watch tonight?
- His remark really annoyed me yesterday.
- Wonder how the game will go on Saturday.
- I wonder if he/she really likes me?.

Research has consistently shown that distracting, intrusive thoughts during an exam are more detrimental to performance than stressful symptoms such as sweaty palms, dry mouth, tension, trembling, etc. Moreover, it does not matter whether the distracting thoughts are negative evaluations related to the exam or are totally irrelevant to the exam. The latter may be a form of escape from the stressful situation.

Checklist: Practical suggestions for controlling wandering thoughts

- ✓ Be aware that this problem is detrimental to performance.
- ✓ Do not look around to find distractions.
- ✓ If distracted, write down 'keep focused on task'.
- ✓ If distracted again, look back at above and continue to do this.
- ✓ Start to draft rough work as soon as you can.
- ✓ If you struggle with initial focus then re-read or elaborate on your rough work.
- ✓ If you have begun your essay, re-read your last paragraph (or two).
- ✓ Do not throw fuel on your distracting thoughts – starve them by re-engaging with the task at hand.

Links to revision

If you have followed the guidelines given for revision, you will be well equipped with outline plans when you enter the exam room. You may have chosen to use headings and subheadings, mind-maps, hierarchical approaches or just a series of simple mnemonics. Whatever method you choose, you should have a series of memory triggers that will help you once you begin to write.

> *Although you may have clear templates with a definite structure or framework for organising your material, you will need to be flexible about how this should be applied to your exam questions.*

For example, imagine that research methods in developmental psychology are one of the topics that you will be examined on. You decide to memorise a list of the methods that might be used, including:

- case study
- experiments
- experimental method
- interviews
- longitudinal research
- observation
- questionnaires

The basic mental template might be these, and a few other categories (such as reliability and validity and ethics). You know that you will not need every last detail, although you may need to select a few from each category. For example you might be asked to:

(a) Outline and evaluate the research methods employed by developmental psychologists.
(b) Consider the special ethical issues involved in developmental psychology.
(c) Discuss the reliability and validity of research methods used to study children.

> *Restrict your material to what is relevant to the question, but bear in mind that this may allow you some scope.*

The art of 'name dropping'

In most topics at university you will be required to cite studies as evidence for your arguments and link these to the names of researchers, scholars or theorists. It will help if you can use the correct dates or at least the decades, and it is good to demonstrate that you have used contemporary sources, and have done some independent work. A marker will have dozens, if not hundreds, of scripts to work through and they will know if you are just repeating the same phrases from the same sources as everyone else. There is inevitably a certain amount of this that will go on, but there is room for you to add fresh and original touches that demonstrate independence and imagination.

Give the clear impression that you have done more than the bare minimum and that you have enthusiasm for the subject. Also, spread the use of researchers' names across your exam essay rather than compressing them into, for example, the first and last paragraphs.

Flight, fight or freeze

As previously noted, the autonomic nervous system (ANS) is activated when danger or apparent danger is imminent. Of course the threat does not have to be physical – as in the case of an exam, a job interview, a driving test or a TV appearance. Indeed, the ANS can be activated even by anticipation of a future threat. However, the reaction is more likely to be stronger as you enter into the crucial time of testing or challenge. Symptoms may include over-breathing, trembling, headaches, nausea, tension, dry mouth and palpitations. How should we react to these once they have been triggered? A postman might decide to run away from a barking dog and run the risk of being chased and bitten. A second possible response is to freeze on the spot – this might arrest the animal in its tracks, but is no use in an exam situation. In contrast, to fight might not be the best strategy against the dog, but will be more productive in an exam. That is, you are going into the exam room to 'tackle' the questions, and not to run away from the challenge before you.

The final illustration below uses the analogy of archery to demonstrate how you might take control in an exam.

Lessons from archery

- Enter the exam room with a quiver full of arrows – all the points you will need to use.
- Eye up the target board you are to shoot at – choose the exam questions.
- Stand in good position for balance and vision – prepare your time management.
- Prepare your bow and arrow and take aim at the target – keep focused on the task at hand and do not be sidetracked.
- Pull the string of the bow back to get maximum thrust on the arrow – match your points to the appropriate question.
- Aim to hit the board where the best marks are (bull's eye or close) – do not be content with the minimum standard, such as a mere pass.
- Pull out arrows and shoot one after another to gain maximum hits and advantage – do not be content with preparing one or two strong points.
- Make sure your arrows are sharp and the supporting bow and string are firm – choose relevant points and support with evidence.
- Avoid wasted effort by loose and careless shots – do not dress up your essay with unnecessary padding.

EXERCISE

Write your own checklist on the range of combined skills and personal qualities that you will need to be at your best in an exam.

✓ ....

✓ ....

✓ ....

✓ ....

✓ ....

With reference to the above exercise – skills might include such things as critical thinking, time and task management, focus on issues, and quick identification of problems to address. Personal qualities might include factors such as confidence, endurance, resilience and stress control.

3.7

tips on interpreting essay and exam questions

What this section will give you – in addressing exam and essay questions. How to:

- focus on the issues that are relevant and central
- read questions carefully and take account of all the words
- produce a balanced critique in your outline structures
- screen for the key words that will shape your response
- focus on different shades of meaning between 'critique', 'evaluate', 'discuss' and 'compare and contrast'

What do you see?

The suggested explanation for visual illusions is the inappropriate use of cues – that is, we try to interpret three-dimensional figures in the real world with the limitations of a two-dimensional screen (the retina in the eye). We use cues such as shade, texture, size, background, etc., to interpret distance, motion, shape, etc., and we sometimes use these inappropriately. Another visual practice we engage in is to 'fill in the blanks' or join up the lines (as in the case of the nine lines above – which we might assume to be a chair). Our tendency is to impose the nearest similar and familiar template on that which we think we see. The same occurs in the social world – when we are introduced to some-one of a different race we may (wrongly) assume certain things about them. The same can also apply to the way you read exam or essay questions. In these cases you are required to 'fill in the blanks' but what you fill in may be the wrong interpretation of the question. This is especially likely if you have primed yourself to expect certain ques-tions to appear in an exam, but it can also happen in coursework essays. Although examiners do not deliberately design questions to trick you or trip you up, they cannot always prevent you from seeing things that were not designed to be there. When one student was asked what the four seasons were, the response given was, 'salt, pep-per, mustard and vinegar'. This was not quite what the examiner had in mind!

> Go into the exam room, or address the coursework essay well prepared, but be flexible enough to structure your learned material around the slant of the question.

A politician's answer

Politicians are renowned for refusing to answer questions directly or for evading them by raising other questions. A humorous example is that when a politician was asked, 'Is it true that you always answer questions by asking another?', the reply was, 'Who told you that?' Therefore, make sure that you answer the set question, although there may be other questions for further study that arise out of this and that you might want to highlight in your conclusion. As a first principle, you must answer the set question and not another question that you had hoped for in the exam or essay.

Do not leave the examiner feeling like the person who interviews a politician and goes away with the impression that the important issues have been sidestepped.

Example: Discuss the view that physical/motor development is an ongoing process

Directly relevant points:

Developments in

- height and weight
- skeletal versus muscular areas
- the brain and nervous system
- puberty

Less relevant points:

- nature versus nurture
- effect of attachment and sensitivity on the development of the brain

Although some of the points listed in the second list may be relevant to development groups overall, they are not as directly relevant as the key thinkers in this area. However, some of the points could be mentioned briefly without going off at a tangent.

Be ready to resist the wealth of fascinating material at your disposal that is not directly relevant to your question.

Missing your question

A student bitterly complained after an exam that the topic he had revised so thoroughly had not been tested in the exam. The first response to that is that students should always cover enough topics to avoid selling themselves short in the exam – the habit of 'question spotting' is always a risky game to play. However, the reality in the anecdotal example was that the question the student was looking for was there, but he had not seen it. He had expected the question to be couched in certain words and he could not find these when he scanned over the questions in blind panic. Therefore, the simple lesson is always to read over the questions carefully, slowly and thoughtfully. This practice is time well spent.

> *You can miss the question if you restrict yourself to looking for a set form of words and if you do not read over all the words carefully.*

Write it down

If you write down the question you have chosen to address, and perhaps quietly articulate it with your lips, you are more likely to process fully its true meaning and intent. Think of how easy it is to misunderstand a question that has been put to you verbally because you have misinterpreted the tone or emphasis.

> *If you read over the question several times you should be aware of all the key words and will begin to sense the connections between the ideas, and will envisage the possible directions you should take in your response.*

Take the following humorous example:

(a) What is that on the road ahead?
(b) What is that on the road, a head?

Question (a) calls for the identification of an object (what is that?), but question (b) has converted this into an object that suggests there has been a decapitation! Ensure therefore that you understand the direction the question is pointing you in so that you do not go off at a tangent. One word in the question that is not properly attended to can throw you completely off track, as in the following example:

(a) Discuss whether the love of money is the root of all evil.
(b) Discuss whether money is the root of all evil.

These are two completely different questions, as (a) suggests that the real problem with money is inherent in faulty human use – that is, money itself may not be a bad thing if it is used as a servant and not a master. Whereas (b) may suggest that behind every evil act that has ever been committed money is likely to have been implicated somewhere in the motive.

Pursue a critical approach

In psychology you are expected to write critically rather than merely descriptively, although it may be necessary to use some minimal descriptive substance as the raw material for your debate.

Example: To what extent can influences on behaviour be explained by biological/hereditary factors?

Can be explained by biological factors:

- genes
- chromosomes

Cannot be explained by biological factors:

Nurture, including the role of

- parents/family
- peers
- play

is more important and offers an alternative explanation.

Given that the question is about a critical evaluation of the evidence, you would need to address the issues one by one from both standpoints

Analyse the parts

In an effective sports team the end product is always greater than the sum of the parts. Similarly, a good essay cannot be constructed without reference to the parts. Furthermore, the parts will arise as you break down the question into the components it suggests to you. Although the breaking-down of a question into components is not sufficient for an excellent essay, it is a necessary starting point.

To achieve a good response to an exam or essay question, aim to integrate all the individual issues presented in a manner that gives shape and direction to your efforts.

Example: Discuss the view that perception develops as a result of nature or nurture.

Two parts to this question are clearly suggested – nature versus nurture, and you would need to do justice to each in your answer. Other issues that arise in relation to these are left for you to suggest and discuss. Examples might be methods of perceptual development.

> *Give yourself plenty of practice at thinking of questions in this kind of way – both with topics on and not on your course. Topics not on your course that really interest you may be a helpful way to 'break you in' to this critical way of thinking.*

Luchins and learning sets

In a series of experiments, Luchins (1959) allowed children to learn how to solve a problem that involved pouring water from and into a series of jugs of various sizes and shapes. He then gave them other problems that could be solved by following the same sequence. However, when he later gave them another problem that could be solved through a simpler sequence, they went about solving it through the previously learned procedure. In this case the original approach was more difficult but it had become so set in the children's minds that they were blinded to the shorter, more direct route.

Example: How much did the wealthy Scottish man leave behind?

The story is told of a wealthy Scottish man who died, and no one in his village knew how much he had left behind. The issue was debated and gossiped about for some time, but one man claimed that he knew how much the man had left. He teased all the debaters and gossips in the village night after night. Eventually he let his big secret out, and the answer was that the rich man had left 'all of it' behind! No one in the village had been able to work out the mischievous man's little ruse because of the convergent thinking style they used. Some exam questions may require you to be divergent in the way you think (that is, not just one obvious solution to the problem). This may mean being like a detective in the way you investigate and problem solve. The only difference is that you may need to set up the problem as well as the solution!

Get into the habit of 'stepping sideways' and looking at questions from several angles. The best way to do this is by practice, for example on previous exam papers.

Checklist: Ensuring that questions are understood before being fully addressed

✓ Read over the chosen question several times.
✓ Write it down to ensure that it is clear.
✓ Check that you have not omitted any important aspect or point of emphasis.
✓ Ensure that you do not wrongly impose preconceived expectations on the question.
✓ Break the question into parts (dismantle and rebuild).

EXERCISE

Write your own checklist on any additional points of guidance for exams that you have picked up from tutors or textbooks.

....

....

....

....

....

When asked to discuss

Students often ask how much of their own opinion they should include in an essay. In a discussion, when you raise one issue, another one can arise out of it. One tutor used to introduce his lectures by saying that he was going to 'unpack' the arguments. When you unpack an object (such as a new desk that has to be assembled), you first remove the overall packaging, such as a large box, and then proceed to remove the covers from all the component parts. After that you attempt to assemble all the parts, according to the given design, so that they hold together in the intended manner. In a discussion your aim should be not just to identify and define all the parts that contribute, but also to show where they fit (or don't fit) into the overall picture.

Although the word 'discuss' implies some allowance for your opinion, remember that this should be informed opinion rather than groundless speculation. Also, there must be direction, order, structure and end project.

Checklist: Features of a response to a 'discuss' question

✓ Contains a chain of issues that lead into each other in sequence.

✓ Clear shape and direction is unfolded in the progression of the argument.

✓ Underpinned by reference to findings and certainties.

✓ Identification of issues where doubt remains.

✓ Tone of argument may be tentative but should not be vague.

If a critique is requested

One example that might help clarify what is involved in a critique is the hotly debated topic of the physical punishment of children. It would be important in the interest of balance and fairness to present all sides and shades of the argument. You would then look at whether there is available evidence to support each argument, and you might introduce issues that have been coloured by prejudice, tradition, religion and legislation. It would be an aim to identify emotional arguments, arguments based on intuition and to get down to those arguments that really have solid evidence-based support. Finally you would want to flag up where the strongest evidence appears to lie, and you should also identify issues that appear to be inconclusive. It would be expected that you should, if possible, arrive at some certainties.

EXERCISE

Write your own summary checklist for the features of a critique. You can either summarise the above points, or use your own points or a mixture of the two.

....

....

....

....

....

If asked to compare and contrast

When asked to compare and contrast, you should be thinking in terms of similarities and differences. You should ask what the two issues have in common, and what features of each are distinct. Your preferred strategy for tackling this might be to work first through all the similarities and then through all the contrasts (or vice versa). On the other hand, you could work through one similarity and contrast, followed by another similarity and contrast, etc.

Example: Write an essay that compares and contrasts theories of the developing self.

1 *Similarities between theories*

   (a) It is agreed that there are different types of self.
   (b) Different stages are proposed in self-formation.

2 *Differences between theories*

   (a) Role of cognitions.
   (b) Ages that developments occur.

> *When you compare and contrast you should aim to paint a true picture of the full 'landscape'.*

Whenever evaluation is requested

A worked example of evaluation – TV soap opera director

Imagine that you are a TV director for a popular soap opera. You have observed in recent months that you have lost some viewers to an alternative soap opera on a rival channel. All is not yet lost because you still have a loyal hard-core of viewers who have remained faithful. Your programme has been broadcast for 10 years and there has, until recently, been little change in viewing figures. The rival programme has used some fresh ideas and new actors and has a big novelty appeal. It will take time to see if their level of viewing can be sustained, but you run the risk that you might lose some more viewers at least in the short term. On the other hand, with some imagination you might be able to attract some viewers back. However, there have been some recent murmurings about aspects of the programme being stale, repetitive and predictable. You have been given the task of evaluating the programme to see if you can ascertain why you have retained the faithful but lost other viewers, and what you could do to improve the programme without compromising the aspects that work. In your task you might want to review past features (retrospective), outline present features (perspective) and envisage positive future changes (prospective). This illustration may provoke you to think about how you might approach a question that asks you to evaluate some theory or concept in your own academic field of study. Some summary points to guide you are presented below:

- Has the theory/concept stood the test of time?
- Is there a supportive evidence base that would not easily be overturned?
- Are there questionable elements that have been or should be challenged?
- Does more recent evidence point to a need for modification?
- Is the theory/concept robust and likely to be around for the foreseeable future?
- Could it be strengthened through being merged with other theories/concepts?

EXERCISE

Write your own checklist on what you remember or understand about each of the following: 'Discuss', 'Compare and Contract', 'Evaluate' and 'critique' (just a key word or two for each). If you find this difficult, you should read the section again and then try the exercise.

....

....

....

....

....

It should be noted that the words presented in the above examples might not always be the exact words that will appear on your exam script – e.g. you might find 'analyse', or 'outline' or 'investigate' etc. The best advice is to check over your past exam papers and familiarise yourself with the words that are most recurrent.

3.8	
summary	

In summary, this section has been designed to give you reference points to measure where you are in your studies, and to help you map out the way ahead in manageable increments. It should now be clear that learning should not merely be a mechanical exercise, such as just memorising and reproducing study material. Quality learning also involves making connections between ideas, thinking at a deeper level by attempting to understand your material and developing a critical approach to learning. However, this cannot be achieved without the discipline of preparation for lectures, seminars and exams, or without learning to structure your material (headings and subheadings) and to set each unit of learning within its overall context in your subject and programme. An important device in learning is to develop the ability to ask questions (whether written, spoken or silent). Another useful device in learning is to illustrate your material and use examples that will help make your study fun, memorable and vivid. It is useful to set problems for yourself that will allow you to think through solutions and therefore enhance the quality of your learning.

On the one hand, there are the necessary disciplined procedures such as preparation before each learning activity and consolidation afterwards. It is also vital to keep your subject materials in organised folders so that you can add/extract/replace materials when you need to. On the other hand, there is the need to develop personality qualities such as feeding your confidence, fuelling your motivation and turning stress responses to your advantage. This section has presented strategies to guide you through finding the balance between these organised and dynamic aspects of academic life.

Your aim should be to become an 'all round student' who engages in and benefits from all the learning activities available to you (lectures, seminars, tutorials, computing, labs, discussions, library work, etc.), and to develop all the academic and personal skills that will put you in the driving seat to academic achievement. It will be motivating and confidence building for you if you can recognise the value of these qualities, both across your academic programme and beyond graduation to the world of work. They will also serve you well in your continued commitment to life-long learning.

Textbook Guide

MCILROY, D. (2003) *Studying at University: How to be a Successful Student.* London: Sage.

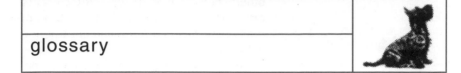

glossary

Accommodation
Involves changing existing schemas to fit the world.

Affectionless psychopathy
This was a term used by Bowlby in his 44 thieves study and is a condition in which individuals are unable to establish normal emotional development. They lack any feelings of emotion or guilt if carrying out crimes, they lack affection and are unable to establish lasting relationships as adults.

Ambiguous questions
People may not give a true response if they are unclear about what a question means.

Animistic thinking
The belief that inanimate objects are alive.

Apgar score
A test to establish basic physical condition of a new born baby. A score is given to indicate heart-rate, respiration, colour, muscle tone and reflexes, to determine whether or not further attention needs to be given to these areas in the postnatal period.

Assimilation
Where the child fits the world into existing schemas.

Attachment (secure and insecure types)
Attachment is a special emotional bond between a child and its caregiver/s. Some believe this occurs with just one person/ the mother (a monotrophic bond) and

others believe that multiple attachments are possible. There are two types of attachment: a secure attachment where a baby shows some distress when separated from its caregiver but is able to continue to play and is readily comforted upon the caregiver's return. Insecure attachments are demonstrated when the child displays resistant or avoidant behaviour following separation from the caregiver. A secure attachment provides the child with a stable and secure base from which to explore the world and is believed to be as important for emotional development as vitamins and proteins are for physical development.

Authoritarian parental style

Restrictive parenting, which expects obedience to set rules.

Authoritative parental style

Restrictions are imposed and child is expected to obey them, but these are explained and meaningful. Parents are responsive to the child's needs.

Autosomal abnormalities

Occur when an abnormal sperm or ovum carrying an extra autosome combines with a normal gamete to form a zygote that has 47 chromosomes, so a trisomy occurs (it contains three chromosomes of that type).

Babbling

The use of vocalisation without particular meaning, although showing speech-like sounds.

Behavioural comparisons phase

In Barenboim's (1981) developmental stages of impression formation this refers to behaviours which are compared to give a sense of self and define others (6–8 years).

Behavioural genetics

Attempts to understand both the genetic and environmental contributions to individual variations in human behaviour.

Behavioural methods

Examine if behaviour changes in response to what is being perceived.

Biometric model

Data from different familial relationships can be combined in a comprehensive model that includes both genetic and environmental influences and, in more complex versions, genotype–environment correlation and interaction.

Biosocial theory

Biological factors and the contribution of social factors that result from interpretations of this.

Bowlby's theory of attachment

The adult/caregiver is genetically pro grammed to form an attachment with the infant in order to protect it. The attachment gives children the opportunity to be around adults and therefore provides asafe base from which the infant can explore the world. The attachment develops between the infant and caregiver because the infant displays 'social releasers' – these are behaviours that elicit/produce a reaction from the caregiver, and include crying, smiling, etc. Attachment is a biological (innate) process and there is a *critical period* of development. This means that if the attachment is not formed within the first 2.5 years, it will not occur at all. In attachment a 'monotrophic bond' is formed – that is a special bond with just one other person. The mother is therefore unique. Bowlby believes that if this bond is not formed, or is broken, then there would be permanent emotional damage, because children only develop socially and emotionally when an attachment provides them with feelings of security. High self-esteem and emotional and social development are therefore derived from having a sensitive, emotionally responsive and supportive caregiver with whom the child has developed an attachment (the internal working model). If the child does not have an attachment then they will not develop emotionally (maternal deprivation hypothesis). Affectionless psychopathy may result where there is a lack of emotional development, a lack of concern for others, a lack of guilt and an inability to form lasting relationships.

Bruner's theory of language (1975)

Stated that the form of language is related to the social world and the routines that take place within it as society helps provide a context for the meaning of words.

Canalisation

Waddington (1966) – where genes operate in such a way that they limit or restrict development to a small number of outcomes.

Case studies

Focus on one individual or small group and their behaviour, thoughts, feelings and experiences.

Centration

The child can only classify things on the basis of a single attribute.

Cephalocaudal development

That is, physical maturation and growth extends from top to toes.

Child-effects model of genetic transmission (Reiss 1997)

Suggests that genes cause certain behaviour in the child, which then causes the parent's reaction. In this model, what the parent does does *not* matter in the development of behaviour.

Chomsky's nativist theory of language (1959)	He believed that language acquisition was innate and that children automatically learn it because they have an inbuilt mechanism that allows them to interpret / de-code the language they hear and its rules.
Chromosomal abnormalities	Are usually the result of an uneven segregation of chromosomes during mitosis and meiosis.
Clinical interviews	Frequently used in developmental psychology, these are semi-structured, so account for the individual while testing a general assumption / hypothesis.
Cognitive-developmental theory	As cognition matures, so does the child's understanding of gender.
Cognitive-developmental theory of attachment	Attachment depends on intellectual development. The infant must be capable, at a cognitive level, of distinguishing between familiar and unfamiliar people and recognising that key attachment figures are permanent even in their absence (object permanence).
Cognitive psychology	Deals with topics such as perception, memory, attention, language, and thinking/ decision-making. Most critically it is based on the idea that we are like a computer when processing information and have input, storage and retrieval functions.
Cohort effects	Are the effects that occur because the social change experienced by a group of varying ages may alter what is found.

Comparative psychology

The comparison between animal and human behaviour underlies this area of psychology, especially the debate between the inheritance of species-specific behaviour patterns (phylogeny) and those which are acquired during the species lifetime but are not shared with every member.

Complex questions

If questions are too long, with too many concepts or technical language, participants may misunderstand and therefore not give a true reflection of their views.

Concrete-operational stage (7–11 years)

The main features of this stage are the acquisition of *reversible thinking, the ability to centre, classification* and *seriation.* Thus the child is able to think backwards mentally, is less egocentric, capable of grouping objects together logically in terms of their common characteristics and able to arrange items in rank order in terms of colour or size (for example).

Concurrent validity

If the test replicates an established one and results correlate, then it must be valid.

Confidentiality

Participants must be assured that all information gained during investigations will be kept confidential as required by the Data Protection Act, and that publication of any findings will not allow them to be subsequently identified.

Construct validity

The test must support the underlying constructs it is measuring (for example, if a person has high blood pressure induced by anxiety then an anxiety questionnaire should support this).

Correlations	Measures the strength of the relationship between two variables; for example, it tests if there is a relationship between two things. It *does not,* however, test cause and effect – so it does not say that one thing causes the other but simply that there is some relationship between the two things.
Cross-sectional research	Studies children of varying ages simultaneously.
Cystic fibrosis	The child lacks an enzyme that prevents mucus from obstructing the lungs and digestive tract.
Debriefing	While debriefing does not justify unethical practices it is used to further the participants understanding of the research aims and processes in which they have taken part. This is to ensure that they do not later suffer any psychological harm from their participation and allows them to gain a full understanding of what procedures have been used, and why, and what results were then obtained.
Deception	It is unethical to deceive/mislead/withhold information from participants, knowingly or unknowingly, about the aims or procedures of any research, unless there is strong scientific justification agreed by an ethics committee.
Demand characteristics	This is where the participant works out the aim of the study and therefore behaves differently (either to please the experimenter or to spoil the study).
Dependent variable	Is what one hopes alters as a result of what is *changed* (so the DV measures any changes the IV has produced).

Deprivation	Bowlby believed that maternal deprivation occurs when the bond between a mother and child is broken in some way (such as mother attending hospital). The child therefore loses the attachment it has formed and Bowlby believed this results in lasting and permanent damage. In the short term the effects of deprivation include protest, despair and detachment, but in the long term maternal deprivation can lead to affectionless psychopathy, which means the child does not show normal emotions (such as guilt) and has difficulty forming lasting relationships.
Developmental psychology	Looks at the changes we go through as we get older and examines the key stages that influence all aspects of our development, from that of the foetus, through infancy and then transitions into adolescence and adulthood. It covers a range of developmental areas including physical, social, emotional, cognitive and language development, as well as relationships with other social agents such as peers and family.
Differentiation theory – perceptual development	Perception develops once distinctive features of objects can be transferred across situations and once they can be differentiated from irrelevant stimuli. Such differentiation tends to occur as a product of age.
Double-barrelled questions	The participant is asked two different questions at once.
Down syndrome	An extra twenty-first chromosome causes this abnormality. Some retardation.
Echoic response	The child tries to repeat something it has just heard.
Ecological validity	Can the method be applied to real-life situations and therefore does it measure naturally occurring behaviour?
Egocentrism	The baby can only see the world from its own perspective and thinks that people see the world in the same way he does, thus failing to distinguish between himself and the rest of the world.

Emotive questions	Rely on emotional appeal and may encourage participants to give an answer that reflects their emotion at the time, or may lead to social desirability bias.
Enactive stage of cognitive development (0–1 year)	At first babies represent the world through actions, and any knowledge is based upon what they have experienced through their own behaviour. Past events are represented through appropriate motor responses and through repeated encounters with the environment automatic patterns emerge.
Enrichment theory	Originally infants develop their sensory and motor abilities in the sensori-motor stage occurring before the age of 2, and interaction with the world aids the development of innate schemas after which new ones can be formed through the process of accommodation. Perception therefore occurs because it is influenced by the expectations that result from such schemas.
Ethical guidelines	A set of guidelines which protect participants who take part in research projects. They include guidelines on consent, deception, debriefing, withdrawal from investigations, confidentiality and the protection of participants from psychological and physical harm.
Ethics	There are also a number of ethical issues that a psychologist should bear in mind when studying children. Principally the guidelines issued by the Society for Research in Child Development (SRCD) must be followed.
Ethology	Attachments are biological. We are born with 'signals' that have evolved to encourage attachment, so it is an evolutionary process that ensures survival. It is an instinct, and Lorenz (1937) found that animals will 'imprint' (follow

the attachment object instinctively from birth) during a critical period, and that this is automatic and irreversible.

Experimenter expectancy (a type of investigator effect)	This is where the expectations of the researcher influence the results by the reseacher either consciously or unconsciously revealing the desired outcome through procedural or recording bias.
Expressive style of language development	Children using action words and people's names.
External reliabilty	Tests the reliability of a method over time.
Eye movement	Eye movements are tracked.
Face/content validity	On the face of it, does the content of the test look like it measures what it claims to?
Factual questions	If a fact is given it is difficult for participants to disagree with the statement, but may not actually indicate that they agree with it.
Family studies	Studies of twins and adoptees, using techniques designed to sort biological from environmental influences. The idea behind this is that if a characteristic is due to hereditary factors then similarity should increase with kinship.
Field experiment	The researcher deliberately manipulates the IV but does so in the participant's own natural environment.
Fixed-choice/closed-ended questions	These are questions to which limited answers are available, for example, yes/no or on a scale from 'strongly disagree' to 'strongly agree'.
Formal-operational stage (11–15 years)	Here the individual shows an ability to reason in the abstract without having to rely on concrete objects/events and the child's thinking resembles that of an adult.

Fragile-X syndrome

The X chromosome is compressed or broken leading to this sex chromosome abnormality. Can cause mental retardation in males.

Fully structured interviews

Here the interview follows a fixed format. The questions are often closed-ended – that is they have a fixed response.

Gender

Refers to the psychological characteristics associated with being male or female.

Gender identity

Goes beyond the biological aspects and focuses more on the awareness of being male or female and will include aspects of gender role (expectations about gender-appropriate behaviours) based partially on stereotypes.

Gender role

Expectations about gender-appropriate behaviours based partially on stereotypes.

Gender schema theory

The child's recognition that there is a difference between males and females which helps them develop schemas or 'theories' about gender-appropriate behaviour, reward and punishment, or vicarious learning (observation).

General symbolic function

The use of mental images, words and other symbols to represent the world.

Genetic defects

Can be caused by recessive genes or mutations where a change in the chemical structure or arrangement of one or more genes produces a new phenotype.

Genetic determinism

The belief that genetics is the major factor in determining behaviour.

Genotype

Our inherited and unique combination of genes.

Glia
Nerve cells that nourish neurons and encase them in insulation.

Habituation
Something is presented to an infant and the time spent looking at it before moving on to something else is measured (that is, until the infant has shown habituation). If he/she has moved on to a second stimulus it indicates perception has taken place, as he/she has shown discrimination between the two.

Haemophilia
The child lacks a substance that causes the blood to clot. Mainly occurs in males.

Holophrastic stage of language development
The stage of one-word development.

Hypothesis
A precise, testable statement of a relationship between two or more variables.

Iconic stage of cognitive development (1–6 years)
Is concerned with images, and this form of representation involves building up a mental image of things we have experienced and such images are usually made up of past encounters with similar objects or situations.

Independent groups
Different participants are used in each condition of the experiment.

Independent variable
This is the thing that the researcher *deliberately manipulates* so it is the thing that she purposely changes.

Informal but guided interviews
The interview is informal but the interviewer may have a list of topics that could be covered.

Informal/ non-directive interviews
Overall aim is to gather data. The person can talk about anything they choose. The

psychologist has no influence on the topics the person wishes to discuss, but may help and guide the discussion in order to increase the individual's self-awareness.

Information Processing Approach (IPA)

According to this approach the human mind is like a computer, or an information processing system capable of the input, storage, retrieval and output of information. Three stages are involved: input from an external stimulus or problem, followed by a decision about the application of the appropriate system for this problem and, lastly, the output response or action. Such processes are automatic and as the brain matures information is transferred to neurons faster. So, processing speed increases as a result of such maturation but also because of experience, for example, regarding the organisation of information.

Informed consent

All participants in scientific research are required to give consent (or in the case of children or other vulnerable groups this must be given on their behalf) and this entails informing them of the demands, objectives and possible effects of the study. It is believed that only after gaining such information can a participant make an informed decision concerning their willingness to participate.

Internal reliability

Refers to how consistent a method measures within itself, a process helped by standardisation (using the same process with each participant).

Inter-rater reliability

The comparison of observations between researchers to ensure they are reliable.

Interviews

These are similar to questionnaires although conducted verbally. Quantitative data (giving responses which can be statistically classified) or qualitative (descriptive in nature) may be collected. Interviews range from being informal through to being fully structured.

Intuitive stage of cognitive development (4–7 years)

There is a limited ability to think logically and on class inclusion tasks the child fails to understand the relationship between superordinate and subordinate classes.

Klinefelter syndrome

Occurs with an imbalance in X chromosomes where two X from the ovum combine with a Y-bearing sperm. The person is phenotypically male but with some female characteristics.

Laboratory experiment

The researcher deliberately exercises strict control over extraneous and confounding variables, using standardised procedures.

Language acquisition device

A device allowing innate language acquisition through an inbuilt mechanism that allows children to interpret/de-code the language they hear and its rules.

Lateralisation

Specialism of brain functions by either the left or right hemisphere.

Leading questions

Lead people into giving the socially desirable answer.

Learning theory of attachment

Attachment is a *learned process* (due to nurture). Infants attach because of classical conditioning – they attach to the mother because she is associated with providing food and attention. So the infant learns to attach to this person based on the associations that are made. Learning theory suggests that a child learns to form an attachment because they experience a desire for food as soon as they are born. They have a need to reduce the drive state (so, to be fed). This is a primary drive because it is innate and arises from a biological need. The child therefore soon learns that food is a reward (it stops them being hungry). This is called a primary reinforcer. Quickly the mother becomes a secondary reinforcer because the child associates her with the food. However, the mother also offers security and contact comfort. She is warm, sensitive and responsive and therefore a secondary drive is created by which the child seeks the mother because she is comforting. Attachment is a two-way process because when the child also responds to the mother (for example 'coo', smiling) the mother will seek repeated interaction, often during the feeding process in the first stage of a child's life.

Longitudinal research

Studies data from individuals over a longer time period.

'Looking-glass self'

Cooley (1902) and Mead (1934) believed that our sense of identity is simply a reflection of how we believe other people see us and indeed how other people respond to us.

MacArthur communicative development inventories

Checklists examining development from 8–28 months old using infant and toddler scales, focusing on early gestures and then word production.

Mand

A word that has personal significance for a child.

Matched pairs	Like independent groups but participants are matched as closely as possible for any factors important for the study – so different but similar people are used.
Maternal deprivation hypothesis	According to Bowlby's maternal deprivation hypothesis an attachment is a two-way, genetic process that provides a child with a secure base from which to explore the world. He therefore stated that if maternal deprivation occurs and the bond is broken in some way then there would be irreversible long-term consequences for the child. This includes affectionless psychopathy where the individual is unable to establish normal emotional development, lacking any feelings of emotion or guilt if carrying out crimes, lacking affection and being unable to establish lasting relationships as adults.
Maturation	Genetic sequence of physical growth that is common to all members of the species.
Menarche	First menstrual period.
MLU	Mean length of utterances.
Morphology	The form or structure of words.
Muscular dystrophy	A disease which attacks the muscles, resulting in loss of motor abilities and affecting speech.
Myelinisation	Neurons become encased in myelin sheaths that allow for the faster transmission of neural impulses.
Natural experiment	The IV is changed by natural occurrence – the researcher just records the effect on the DV.

Naturalistic observation	People are observed in their natural environment.
Neurons	Nerve cells that receive and transmit neural impulses.
Object permanence	Is where a baby understands that objects continue to exist even when they are not being perceived or manipulated in some way.
Observations	Look at the behaviour of participants in various situations and see 'a relatively unconstrained segment of a person's freely chosen behaviour as it occurs' (Coolican, 1990). These can be structured or unstructured but can be carried out in the participant's natural environment.
Observer bias	Experimenter/observer expectancy in which each observer differs in the way they perceive, value and label behaviour, which results in a bias.
Open-ended questions	These allow participants to contribute their own views to a question where a number of answers may be given.
Over-generalisation	Rules are used in situations in which they do not apply.
Parent-effects model of genetic transmission (Reiss, 1997)	A model which suggests that genes cause the child's temperament, which in turn causes the parent's response, which results in certain behaviour in the child. In this model, what the parent does *does* matter in the development of behaviour.
Participant observation	Observes participants in their natural environment but observer participates in the group being studied.

Perceptual development	'Perceptual development is the growth of interpretive skills – a complex process that depends, in part, on the expression of individual genotypes, the maturation of the sensory receptors, the kinds of sensory experiences that the child has available to analyse and interpret, the child's emerging cognitive abilities, and the social context in which all these other variables operate' (D.R. Shaffer, 1993).
Permissive parental style	Freedom of expression and behaviour is permitted with few demands or rules imposed on the child.
Phenotype	The observable physical or biochemical characteristics of an organism.
Phenylketonuria	The enzyme necessary to digest foods is lacking. Can cause retardation and hyperactivity if not treated.
Phonology	The study of the system of sounds in a language.
Pincer grip	The thumb is used in opposition to the fingers, facilitating better manipulation of objects.
Pivot words	Words that tend to appear in the same place in speech.
Plasticity	Capacity for change.
Pragmatics	Information regarding the rules of language.
Pre-conceptual stage (2–4 years)	The child's thinking makes it difficult for it to understand relative terms, for example, 'bigger' rather than 'big' or 'biggest'. The child can only classify things on the basis

of a single attribute (*centration*) and has difficulty with *seriation*, that is, the arrangement of objects on the basis of a particular dimension.

Predictive validity

If a test accurately predicts future performance (for example, good GCSE scores indicate good AS results) then it is said to be valid.

Preference methods

A child's preference for one stimulus over another is simply observed (longer looking time is taken as a preference for that stimulus).

Prelinguistic stage of language development

The most important aspect of which is babbling.

Pre-operational stage (2–7 years)

In this stage the child is still largely influenced by the way objects look/how they seem rather than by any particular logic.

Preschool language development

Where speech becomes longer, more complex and contains more grammatical morphemes including prepositions, prefixes and suffixes.

Primary circular reactions

The sense of self is focused on pleasure in body functions/movements.

*Private self

'Those inner, or subjective, aspects of self that are known only to the individual and are not available for public scrutiny' (D.R. Shaffer, 1993: 437).

Privation

The child has never had the opportunity to establish an attachment with an appropriate caregiver (if, for example, they are orphaned). Unlike deprivation they have not lost the attachment but have never formed it in the beginning. This was believed to have many long-term consequences for emotional and social development, although some studies have shown that this will depend on the substitute care offered to the child. It is possible that a child who has suffered privation will develop well within a caring (substituted) family environment but still have difficulties establishing relationships with adults outside of the family setting.

Protection of participants from harm

During the course of research participants should not be subjected to any risk of harm beyond that they would normally expect from their lifestyle. Psychologists must prioritise the safety and physical/psychological well-being of their participants above all else.

Proximo-distal development

Growth extends from the centre of the body outwards.

Psychological comparisons phase

In Barenboim's (1981) developmental stages of impression formation this is where a process of comparing and contrasting takes place (12–16 years).

Psychological constructs phase

In Barenboim's (1981) developmental stages of impression formation this sees that stable traits of self and others are now considered (8/9–10/11 years).

Puberty

Development that marks sexual maturity.

Public self

'Those aspects of self that others can see or infer' (D.R. Shaffer, 1993: 437).

QTL analysis

The development of genetic linkage maps means that attention is now focused on the identification of susceptibility genes for common, complex disorders.

Quasi experiment	Any experiment in which control is lacking over the IV.
Questionnaires	Use various types of questions to make a quick and efficient assessment of people's attitudes and which contain fixed or open-ended questions (or both).
Range-of-reaction principle (Gottesman, 1963)	Suggests that one's genotype sets limits on the range of phenotypes one could possibly exhibit in response to different environments.
Referential style of language development	Object names are used.
Reliability	A test is reliable if it measures a variable consistently.
Repeated measures	The same participants are used in each condition of the experiment.
Rouge test (Lewis & Brooks-Gunn, 1979)	One way of assessing the development of self is to apply a spot of rouge to a child and then place them in front of a mirror. If the child tries to rub it off themselves, rather than off the reflection, it can be assumed that they have acquired a sense of self-recognition.
Scaffolding	The support/context the adult provides for the child.
Schema	An internal representation of a specific physical or mental action. Schemas change through a process of assimilation and accommodation.
Scientific method	Means that you need to test a hypothesis to examine variables that influence behaviour. Thus, the hypothesis states that two variables are related in some way and if you alter one of them this may cause the participant

to alter the other. In psychology we are trying to show that our results are significant and due to the thing we have changed (called the independent variable) rather than due to chance.

Secondary circular reactions

Repetition of actions that interact with the environment and are external to the self, which ocour at 4–8 months, when the infant's attention is focused on objects outside the body.

Selective breeding

Researchers try to selectively breed certain attributes in animals.

Self-esteem

'A person's feelings about the qualities and characteristics that make up his or her self concept' (D.R. Shaffer, 1993: 439).

Selman (1980) – stages of social perspective taking

According to Selman a sense of self and identity can only develop once a child understands others and can discriminate between different perspectives. He proposed five different stages: egocentric or undifferentiated perspective (3–6 years); social-informational role-taking (6–8 years); self-reflective role-taking (8–10 years); mutual role-taking (10–12 years); social and conventional system role-taking (12–15 years+).

Semantics

The science of the meaning of words.

Sensorimotor stage (0–2 years)

The child experiences the world (mainly) through its immediate perceptual and physical (sensory and motor) abilities.

Primary circular reactions

Emerge at 1–4 months where basic reflex or motor movements are made as a function of one's own body.

Seriation	The arrangement of objects on the basis of a particular dimension.
Shape constancy	An object is seen as the same shape despite orientation.
Size constancy	An object is seen as a constant size despite its changing size in the retinal image.
Skinner's learning theory of language (1957)	Skinner saw language merely as a product of trial and error, reinforcement and behaviour shaping.
Social agents	Parents, peers, school, etc., for example.
Social desirability bias	This is where the participant tries to 'look good' or respond in a socially desirable way.
Social psychology	Social psychology is about understanding individual behaviour in a social context. Baron, Byrne & Suls (1989) define it as 'the scientific field that seeks to understand the nature and causes of individual behaviour in social situations'. It therefore looks at human behaviour as influenced by other people and the context in which this occurs.
Social referencing	Being able to interpret someone else's emotions before deciding one's own emotional expression.
Socialisation	Refers to the process by which the individual child adapts to the social order into which it is born and is the means by which the child becomes a full participating member of society.
Sociobiological theory	A theory which states that genes are passed on through evolution thus male and female

behave and look different because such behaviour is adaptive and these differences maximise reproduction and ensure survival of the genes.

Split-half method

Where a test (e.g., on stress) is split in half and the scores on each half are then calculated. If the results indicate consistency (and correlate) it is assumed that the test is reliable.

Stages of attachment

Schaffer and Emerson (1964) believe that attachments form in stages: 0–2 months where infants display pre-attachment behaviour showing similar responses to all objects; an indiscriminate attachment phase developing at 2–7 months where infants start to distinguish familiar and unfamiliar people; a specific attachment then develops at 7–24 months and this is marked by separation protest and stranger anxiety; and lastly multiple attachments are formed from 8 months onwards.

Stimulus seeking

The infant simply has a biological urge to scan the environment and explore any stimuli he can see well.

Strange situation

Ainsworth and Bell (1970) devised a method for testing the type and security of attachments a child was experiencing. It is an experimental procedure consisting of seven steps, which looks at the behaviour of the infant when separated from the mother (e.g., how do they react? do they continue to play with toys?), their behaviour in the presence of a stranger and their response upon the mother's return. Two specific areas are measured – a child's separation anxiety (how anxious do they become when the mother leaves them behind) and stranger anxiety (how anxious do they respond to a stranger when left alone with them). From this Ainsworth and Bell believed you could categorise a child's attachment behaviour as either secure (distress is shown on separation but upon reunion with the mother behaviour returns to normal; the mother's company is preferred to that of a stranger) or insecure. If the child shows an insecure resistant attachment type they are distressed upon separation but when the mother returns resist efforts to comfort them and are wary of the stranger. In contrast an insecure anxious child does not react to either the mother leaving or returning and equally avoids the stranger.

Structured but open-ended interviews	Use a standardised procedure where the interviewer asks pre-set questions. The interviewee can still express how they feel if they are given open-ended questions.
Structured observation	Is structured so that observers classify behaviour in set ways.
Syncretic reasoning	The linking of neighbouring objects or events together on the basis of common elements.
Syntax	The grammatical structure of sentences.
Tact	The child may be rewarded for similar production of a word to one they have heard.
Telegraphic stage of language development	Where two-word phrases are produced involving nouns and verbs but excluding function words ('a'), plurals and tenses.
Test–re-test method	Where you carry out the test on more than one occasion (with the same participant) and

if scores are consistent (and correlate) then it is assumed to be reliable.

The passive model of genetic transmission (Reiss, 1997)

Genetic effects are attributed to the 50 per cent overlap in genes between a parent and biological child.

Theory of mind

Is concerned with the way we assess and theorise about the mental states of others and theory of mind is usually tested using false belief tasks. Here a child is given a scenario and is judged according to whether or not they will apply a knowingly incorrect decision themselves, or show awareness of another acting 'incorrectly'.

Transductive reasoning

Incorrect inferences are drawn about the relationship between two objects based on a single attribute.

Turner's syndrome

Occurs when an ovum containing no X chromosome is fertilised by an X-bearing sperm. Phenotypically female but infertile.

Ulnar grasp

Using fingers against the palm to hold objects.

Validity

A test is valid if it measures what it is supposed to and if variables are therefore operationalised (clearly defined so that they are measurable)

Visual cliff

A 'visual cliff', which was actually a table top with glass, was designed whereby a check pattern was placed under one side (shallow end) and on the floor beneath the top on the other (deep end). Results found that babies (6.5–12 months) were reluctant to crawl on to the deep side, thus supporting the idea that depth cues are innate because they are developed even at this age.

Visual preference task

Young infants (4 days to 5 months) were shown discs that were either blank or with features that resembled human facial features either in the correct position or jumbled up. They showed a preference for ones most closely resembling a face.

Visual reinforcement

When the response to a stimulus is evident then the response remains but when the attention decreases it is changed. The idea is that visual response is reinforced in some way by a device the child has control of and can be altered when more reinforcement is needed.

Withdrawal from investigations

Before commencing any research the investigator must assure participants that they may leave the study at any time should they wish to do so, and there is a duty to ensure that the environment permits this. Withdrawal is permitted even if participants have volunteered, or been paid to participate, and even if participants have completed a study but then wish their data to be disregarded.

Zone of proximal development

The difference between a child's actual and potential levels of development – i.e., those functions that have not yet matured but are in the process of maturation.

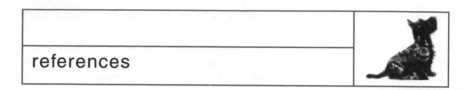

references

Ainsworth, M. D. S., & Bell, S. M. (1970). Attachment, exploration and separation: illustrated by the behaviour of one-year-olds in a Strange Situation. *Child Development, 41*, 49–65.

Anglin, J. M. (1993). Vocabulary development: a morphological analysis. *Monographs of the Society for Research in Child Development, 10*, 238.

Bandura, A. (1977). *Social learning theory.* New York: Prentice-Hall.

Barenboim, C. (1981). The development of person perception in childhood and adolescence. From behavioural comparisons to psychological constructs to psychological comparisons. *Child Development, 52*, 129–144.

Baron-Cohen, S., Leslie, A. M. & Frith, U. (1985). Does the autistic child have a theory of mind? *Cognition, 21*, 37–46.

Baron, R. A., Byrne, D. & Suls, J. (1989). *Exploring social psychology* (3rd ed.) (p. 6). Allyn and Bacon.

Baumrind, D. (1967). Child care practices anteceding three patterns of preschool behaviour. *Genetic Psychology Monographs, 75*, 43–88.

Baumrind, D. (1971). Current patterns of parental authority. *Developmental Psychology Monographs, 4* (1), 2.

Baumrind, D. (1977). Socialisation determinants of personal agency. Paper presented at the biennial meeting of the Society for Research in Child Development, New Orleans.

Bigelow, A. E. (1977). The development of self and recognition in young children. *Dissertation Abstracts International, 37* (12B), 6360–6361.

Blakemore, C. & Cooper, G. F. (1970). Development of the brain depends on the visual environment. *Nature, 228*, 477–478.

Bower, T. G. R. (1966). The visual world of infants. *Scientific American, 215*, 80–92.

Bowlby, J. (1944). Forty-four juvenile thieves: their characters and home lives. *International Journal of Psychoanalysis, 25*, 107–127.

Bowlby, J., Ainsworth, M., Boston, M. & Rosenbluth, D. (1956). The effects of mother-child separation: a follow-up study. *British Journal of Medical Psychology, 29*, 211–247.

Braine, M. D. S. (1963). In M. W. Eysenck, & C. Flanagan (eds) (2001). *Psychology for AS level.* p. 331. Psychology Press: Taylor & Francis Group.

Bronson, W. C. (1985). Growth in the organisation of behaviour over the second year of life. *Developmental Psychology, 21*, 108–117.

Brown, R. (1973). In M. W. Eysenck, & C. Flanagan (eds) (2001). *Psychology for AS level*. p. 331. Psychology Press: Taylor & Francis Group.

Bruner, J. S. (1975). The ontogenesis of speech acts. *Journal of Child Language, 2*, 1–19.

Bruner, J. S. (1983). *Child's talk*. New York: Norton.

Bruner, J. S., Olver, R. R., & Greenfield, A. (1966). *Studies in cognitive growth*. New York: Wiley.

Buhrmester, D. (1996). In M. Harris, & G. Butterworth (eds) (2004). *Developmental psychology: a student's handbook*. p. 315. Psychology Press: Taylor & Francis Group.

Butterworth, G. E., & Cicchetti, D. (1978). Visual calibration of posture in normal and Down's syndrome infants. *Perception, 5*, 155–160.

Cairns, R. B. (1979). In Shayter, D. R. (1993). *Developmental psychology: childhood and adolescence* (3rd ed.). Pacific Grove, CA: Brooks/Cole.

Caron, A. J., Caron, R. F., & Carlson, V. R. (1979). Infant perception of the invariant shape of objects varying in slant. *Child Development, 50*, 716–721.

Chomsky, N. (1959). Review of *Verbal behavior* by B. F. Skinner. *Language, 35*, 26–58.

Chomsky, N. ([1959] 1986). *Knowledge of language: its nature, origin and use*. New York: Praeger.

Clarke, A. M., & Clarke, A. D. B. (1976). *Early experience: myth and evidence*. New York: Free Press.

Cooley, C. H. (1902). *Human nature and the social order*. New York: Scribner's.

Coolican, H. (1990). *Research methods and statistics in psychology* (3rd ed.). London: Hodder & Stoughton.

Coolican, H. (2004). *Research methods and statistics in psychology* (4th ed.). London: Hodder & Stoughton.

Curtiss, S. (1977). In R. D. Gross (2001). *Psychology: the science of mind and behaviour* (4th ed.). p. 285. London: Hodder & Stoughton.

De Casper, A. J., & Spence, M. J. (1986). Prenatal maternal speech influences newborns' perception of speech sounds. *Infant Behaviour & Development, 9*, 133–150.

Eimas, P. (1974). Auditory and linguistic cues for place of articulation by infants. *Perception & Psychophysics, 16*, 513–521.

Eimas, P. D., Siqueland, E., Jusczyk, P., & Vogorito, J. (1971). Speech perception in infants. *Science, 171*, 303–306.

Erikson, E. H. (1963). *Childhood and society* (2nd ed.). New York: Norton.

Fantz, R. L. (1961). The origin of form perception. *Scientific American, 204*, 66–72.

Fenson, L., Dale, P. S., Resnick, J. S., Bates, E., Thal, D. J., & Pethnick, S. J. (1994). Variability in early communicative development. *Monographs of the Society for Research in Child Development, 59*, 173.

Fenson, L., Dale, P. S., Resnick, J. S., Bates, E., Thal, D. J., Reilly, J., & Hartung, J. (1990). In M. Harris, & G. Butterworth (eds) (2004). *Developmental psychology: a student's handbook.* p. 151. Psychology Press: Taylor & Francis Group.

Flavell, J. M. (1963). *The developmental psychology of Jean Piaget.* Princeton, NJ: Van Nostrand.

Freud, S. (1938). Three contributions to the theory of sex. In A. A. Brill (1995). *The basic writings of Sigmund Freud.* New York: Random House.

Ganzer, V. J. (1968). 'Effects of audience presence and test anxiety on learning and retention in a serial learning situation', *Journal of Personality and Social Psychology, 8,* 194–9.

Gibson, E. J., & Walk, R. D. (1960). The visual cliff. *Scientific American, 202,* 64–71.

Gottesman, I. I. (1963). Heritability of personality: a demonstration. *Psychological Monographs, 77* (whole no. 572).

Harlow, H. E., & Zimmerman, R. R. (1959). Affectional responses in the infant monkey. *Science, 130,* 421–432.

Harris, M., & Butterworth, G. (2004). *Developmental psychology: a student's handbook.* Psychology Press: Taylor & Francis Group.

Harris, P. L. (2000). *The work of the imagination.* Oxford, UK: Blackwell.

Harter, S. (1981). A new self-report scale of intrinsic versus extrinsic orientation in the classroom: motivational and informational components. *Developmental Psychology, 17,* 300–312.

Harter, S. (1982). The perceived competence scale for children. *Child Development, 53,* 87–97.

Hartup, W. W. (1983). In D. R. Shaffer (1993). *Developmental psychology: childhood and adolescence* (3rd ed.) p. 625. Pacific Grove, CA: Brooks/Cole.

Hartup, W. W. (1996). In M. Harris, & G. Butterworth (eds) (2004). *Developmental psychology: a student's handbook.* p. 625. Psychology Press: Taylor & Francis Group.

Hazan, C., & Shaver, P. R. (1987). In M. Eysenck, & C. Flanagan (eds) (2000). *Psychology for AS level.* p. 76. Psychology Press: Taylor & Francis Group.

Held, R., & Hein, A. (1963). Movement produced stimulation in the development of visually guided behaviour. *Journal of Comparative and Physiological Psychology, 56,* 872–876.

Hinde, R. A. (1987). *Individuals, relationships and culture.* Cambridge, UK: Cambridge University Press.

Hodges, J. & Tizard, B. (1989). In R. D. Gross, (1994). *Key Studies in Psychology* (2nd ed.) (pp. 253–275). London: Hodder & Stoughton.

Izard, C. E. (1982). *Measuring emotions in infant and children.* New York: Cambridge University Press.

Jacklin, C. N., & Maccoby, E. E. (1978). Social behaviour at 33 months in same-sex and mixed-sex dyads. *Child Development, 49*, 557–569.

Janowsky, J. S., & Finlay, B. L. (1986). The outcome of perinatal brain damage: the role of normal neuron loss and axon retraction. *Developmental Medicine and Child Neurology, 28*, 375–389.

Johnson, W., Emde, R. N., Pannabecker, B., Stenberg, C., & Davis, M. (1982). Maternal perception of infant emotion from birth through 18 months. *Infant Behavior and Development, 5*, 313–322.

Klaus, M. H., & Kennell, J. H. (1976). *Maternal–infant bonding.* St Louis: Mosby.

Kohlberg, L. (1966). A cognitive developmental analysis of children's sex role concepts and attitudes. In M. W. Eysenck, & C. Flanagan (eds) (2001). *Psychology for A2 level* (pp. 431–433). Psychology Press: Taylor & Francis Group.

Koluchova, J. (1972). In R. Gross, (2001). *Psychology: the science of mind and behaviour* (4th ed.). p. 471. London: Hodder & Stoughton.

Lamb, M. E., Easterbrooks, M. A. (1980). Reinforcement and punishment among preschoolers: characteristics, effects and correlates. *Child Development, 51*, 1230–1236.

Lazar, I. & Darlington, R. (1982). Lasting effects of early education: a report from the Consortium of Longitudinal Studies, *Monographs of the Society for Research in Child Development, 47* (2–3), 195.

LeVine, R. A. (1974). Parental goals: a cross cultural view. *Teachers College Record, 76*, 226–239.

Lewis, M. & Brooks-Gunn, J. (1979). *Social cognition and the acquisition of self.* New York: Plenum.

Liben, L. S., & Signorella, M. L. (1993). Gender-schematic processing in children: the role of initial interpretations of stimuli. *Developmental Psychology, 29*, 141–9.

Lorenz, K. Z. (1937). The companion in the bird's world. *Auk, 54*, 245–273.

Maccoby, E. E. (1980). *Social development: psychological growth and the parent–child relationship.* New York: Harcourt Brace Jovanovich.

Main, M & Solomon, J. (1986). Discovery of a disorganised disorientated attachment pattern. In M. W. Eysenck & C. Flanagan (eds.) (2001). *Psychology for A2 level.* Psychology Press: Taylor & Francis Group.

Marcia, J. E. (1966). Development and validation of ego identity status. *Journal of Personality & Social Psychology, 3*, 551–558.

Martin, C. L. & Halverson, C. F. (1983). The effects of sex-typing schemas on young children's memory. *Child Development, 54*, 563–574.

McClelland, D. C., Atkinson, J. W., Clark, R. A. & Lowell, E. L. (1953). *The achievement motive.* East Norwalk CT: Appleton-Century-Crofts.

McIlroy, D. (2003). *Studying at university: How to be a successful student.* London: SAGE.

McInerney, J. D. (1999). Genes and behaviour: a complex relationship. *Judicature, 83,* 112.

McNeill, D. (1970). In M. W. Eysenck, & C. Flanagan (eds) (2001). *Psychology for A2 level.* p. 331. Psychology Press: Taylor & Francis Group.

Mead, G. H. (1934). *Mind, self & society.* Chicago: Chicago University Press.

Mendel, G. (1865). In D. R. Shaffer (1993). *Developmental psychology: childhood and adolescence* (3rd ed.). p. 75. Pacific Grove, CA: Brooks/Cole.

Money, J., & Ehrhardt, A. A. (1972). *Man and woman, boy and girl.* Baltimore: Johns Hopkins University Press.

Morgan, T. S. (1933). In D. R. Shaffer (1993). *Developmental psychology: childhood and adolescence* (3rd ed.). p. 76. Pacific Grove, CA: Brooks/Cole.

Mueller, E. & Vandell, D. I. (1979). Infant – infant interaction. In D. R. Shaffer (1993). *Developmental psychology: childhood and adolescence* (3rd ed.) (p. 450). Pacific Grove, CA: Brooks/Cole.

Nelson, K. (1973). Structure and strategy in learning to talk. *Monographs of the Society for Research in Child Development, 38,* 149.

Oller, D. K. (1980). In M. Harris, & G. Butterworth (eds) (2004). *Developmental psychology: a student's handbook.* p. 147. Psychology Press: Taylor & Francis Group.

Parten, A. (1932, 1933). In S. Dockett, and M. Fleer (1999). *Play and pedagogy in early childhood.* Marrickville, NSW: Harcourt Brace.

Piaget, J. (1952). *The origins of intelligence in children.* New York: International Universities Press.

Piaget, J. (1962). *Play, dreams and imitation in childhood.* New York: Norton.

Piaget, J. (1965). *The moral judgement of the child.* New York: Free Press.

Piaget, J. (1967). *The child's conception of the world.* Totoura, NJ: Littlefield, Adams.

Piaget, J., & Inhelder, B. (1956). *The child's conception of space.* London: Routledge & Kegan Paul.

Plomin, R., DeFries, J. C., & McClearn, G. E. (1980). *Behavioral genetics: a primer.* New York: W. H. Freeman.

Reisen, A. H. (1950). Arrested vision. *Scientific American, 408,* 16–19.

Reiss, D. (1997). Mechanisms linking genetic and social influences in adolescent development: beginning a collaborative search. *Current Directions in Psychological Science, 6,* 100–105.

Robertson, J. & Robertson, J. (1971). Young children in brief separation. *Psychoanalytic Study of the Child, 26,* 264–315.

Rothstein, M. A. (1999). The impact of behavioural genetics on the law and the courts. *Judicature, 83,* 116.

Rotter, J. B. (1966). Generalized expectancies for internal versus external control of reinforcement. *Psychological Monographs, 80*, (whole no. 609).

Rowe, D. C., & Plomin, R. (1981). The importance of non-shared (E1) environmental influences in behavioural development. *Developmental Psychology, 17*, 517–531.

Scarr, S., & McCartney, K. (1983). How people make their own environments: a theory of genotype–environment effects. *Child Development, 54*, 424–435.

Scarr, S., & Weinberg, R. A. (1976). IQ test performance of black children adopted by white families. *American Psychologist, 31*, 726–739.

Scarr, S., & Weinberg, R. A. (1983). The Minnesota adoption studies: genetic differences and malleability. *Child Development, 54* (2), 260–267.

Schacter, S. (1959). *The psychology of affiliation.* Stanford, CA: Stanford University Press.

Schaffer, H. R., & Emerson, P. E. (1964). The development of social attachments in infancy. *Monographs of the Society for Research in Child Development, 29*.

Seligman, M. E. P. (1975). *Helplessness.* San Francisco: Freeman.

Selman, R. L. (1980). *The growth of interpersonal understanding.* Orlando, FL: Academic Press.

Shaffer, D. A. (1993). In M. W. Eysenck, & C. Flanagan (eds) (2001). *Psychology for A2 level.* p. 329. Psychology Press: Taylor & Francis Group.

Shaffer, D. R. (1993). *Developmental psychology: childhood and adolescence* (3rd ed.). Pacific Grove, CA: Brooks/Cole.

Skinner, B. F. (1957). *Verbal behavior.* New York: Appleton-Century-Crofts.

Slabey, R. G., & Frey, K. G. (1975). Development of gender constancy and selective attention to same-sex models. *Child Development, 46*, 849–56.

Smith, C., & Lloyd, B. (1978). Maternal behaviour and perceived sex of the infant: revisited. *Child Development, 49*, (4) 1263–1265.

Stark (1980). In M. Harris, & G. Butterworth (eds) (2004). *Developmental psychology: a student's handbook.* p. 147. Psychology Press: Taylor & Francis Group.

Tanner, J. M. (1978). *Fetus into man: physical growth from conception to maturity.* Cambridge, MA: Harvard University Press.

Van Lieshout, C. F. M., & Doise, W. (1998). In M. Harris, & G. Butterworth (eds) (2004). *Developmental psychology: a student's handbook.* p. 318. Psychology Press: Taylor & Francis Group.

Verenikina, I. M., Harris P. J. & Lysaght P. (2003). Child's play: computer games, theories of play and children's development. *ACM International Conference Proceeding Series*: vol. 98. Proceedings of the international federation for information processing working group 3.5 open conference on young children and learning technologies – Volume 34.

Vygotsky, L. S. (1962). *Thought and language*. Boston: MIT Press.

Vygotsky, L. S. (1978). *Mind in society*. Cambridge, MA: Harvard University Press.

Waddington, C. H. (1966). *Principles of development and differentiation*. New York: Macmillan.

Weiner, B. (1986). *An attributional theory of motivation and emotion*. New York: Springer-Verlag.

White, R. W. (1959). Motivation reconsidered. The concept of competence. *Psychological Review, 66*, 297–333.

Wolff, K. F. (1759/1959). In D. R. Shaffer (1993). *Developmental psychology: childhood and adolescence* (3rd ed.). p. 75. Pacific Grove, CA: Brooks/Cole.